BONEHEADS

BONEHEADS
MY SEARCH FOR T. REX

RICHARD POLSKY

A KANBAR & CONRAD BOOK

COUNCIL
OAK
BOOKS

SAN FRANCISCO & TULSA

www.counciloakbooks.com

First printing, first edition, 2011

Printed in Canada

Cover and interior design by Tom Morgan

LIBRARY OF CONGRESS CATALOGING-IN-PUBLICATION DATA
Polsky, Richard.
 Boneheads : my search for T. rex / by Richard Polsky. ~ 1st ed.
  p. cm.
 ISBN 978-1-57178-253-3 (hardcover : alk. paper) ~ ISBN 978-1-57178-308-0 (ebook)
1. Tyrannosaurus rex~South Dakota. 2. Animals, Fossil~Collectors and collecting~South Dakota. I. Title.

QE862.S3P65 2011
567.912'909783~dc22

2010048230

Hardcover ISBN: 978-1-57178-253-3
Ebook ISBN: 978-1-57178-308-0

FOR BARNABY CONRAD III

CONTENTS

PART ONE

THE ALLURE OF REX

"That rex tooth of yours is expensive for being a bit weathered ..."

"Yeah? How do you think you'd look after 65 million years in the ground?"

— NEGOTIATIONS AT THE TUCSON FOSSIL FAIR

INTRODUCTION

I f you could live your life all over again, would you live it the same way? In my case, the road not taken might have led to a career in paleontology—a life of hunting dinosaur bones, the skeletal remains of the largest creatures ever to roam the earth. Instead, I became an art dealer, pursuing another form of big game—blue chip paintings by contemporary masters. Yet after twenty-five years of stalking pictures at art galleries and auctions, the allure of fossils remained strong.

Suddenly at fifty I found an opportunity to experience life all over again. My business was on automatic pilot. The art world was on hold, a financially burdensome marriage was winding down, and my passion for dinosaurs had soared to a new peak. All the while I had maintained my contacts in the fossil world. I continued to collect, attend shows, and read voraciously about new discoveries. Now I was in a position—financially and emotionally—to get out in the field and look for dinosaurs.

I was ready to join the Boneheads. I wanted to dig with them during the day and drink with them at night. I wanted to fête the femur and toast the tibia. I wanted to share in the glory of the find and commiserate over the one that got away. I wanted to see if this was the career I should have originally pursued before I became a fossil myself.

As a boy, I was fascinated by dinosaurs. By the age of five, I could recite the names of all the well-known species. One day, I glanced at an advertisement on the back of a comic book. A malevolent T. rex stalked its prey with a lava-spewing volcano in the background. For a mere dollar I could be the proud owner of ten genuine fossils. The collection included a horn coral, a trilobite, and a tiny shark tooth. But the real prize was a fragment of bone from the monster depicted in the promotional illustration—a piece of an actual Tyrannosaurus rex.

I truly believed that if I could scrape together a dollar, I could own part of a T. rex. I saved my allowance, a dime at a time, and eventually sent away for the fossils. I was not disappointed. That very week at school, I was a hero during show and tell.

A few days later, I went to visit Cory, a friend who lived in a new sub-division in Livonia, a suburb of Detroit. His backyard was swampland that a developer had begun to fill. A dump truck had recently delivered a large pile of rocks for that purpose. That day, we began flinging them into the water. I grabbed a rock and was about to toss it when I noticed its unusual form. It was a fossilized horn coral.

I began to slide it into my pocket when Cory cried out, "Throw it in!"

"No—it's a fossil," I yelled back.

I'm sure Cory had no idea what I was talking about. He started to grow angry, "I told you to throw it in!"

"It's a fossil—it's valuable. I'm keeping it."

"Then get off my property!"

Calmly pocketing the petrified bit of ancient marine life, I went home secure in the knowledge I had done the right thing.

Little did I know that story would prove to be a metaphor for the paranoia I would encounter in the future when I decided to get serious about collecting. What was it about fossils? It wasn't as if they were alive and could harm anyone. Why did they provoke people and often inspire irrational behavior?

The Boneheads would reveal all.

CHAPTER ONE

The Fossil Trail: From Manhattan to Tucson

F ew things surprise me when it comes to human behavior and the world of collectibles. That changed when I read an article about "Sue," the greatest T. rex ever discovered. The story had it all: money laundering, fossil poaching, the Sioux nation up in arms, a nasty lawsuit, jail time for the T. rex's would-be owner, and millions for its eventual owner, who celebrated at the Waldorf Astoria wearing a cowboy hat. The incident left such an impression on me that I found myself daydreaming about hunting for "thunder lizards."

Then I began to think big: Why not find my own T. rex?

Henry Galiano was a trained paleontologist who left the museum world to form Maxilla & Mandible, a business largely credited with introducing the phenomenon of natural history specimens as decorative objects. Not long after he opened, interior designers turned to meteorites and amethyst geodes to add an exotic touch to Manhattan duplexes and hotel lobbies in Las Vegas. In fact, the growing demand for aesthetically pleasing specimens led to the formation of a new auction house category—Natural History—with Henry serving as a paid consultant to Sotheby's.

Everyone who made Henry's acquaintance liked him. His non-competitive personality put people at ease. Henry was the personification of a rather hip scientist—longish well-groomed

hair, designer glasses, and clothes that actually fit. He often wore
a belt buckle made of sterling silver inlaid with woolly mammoth
ivory. At first glance, you had a hard time placing his ethnicity; he
was of Cuban-Chinese heritage. Yet once he began speaking, you
realized he was just a regular guy who happened to be obsessed
with fossils.

Henry was a fossil missionary in his zeal to spread the word.
His store on Columbus Avenue in Manhattan was prosperous;
yet it was obvious that he wasn't in it for the money. Whenever
I stopped by to make a small purchase, he insisted on offering
me a whopping discount. He instinctively knew that I bought
fossils for the sheer joy of living with them, something he could
easily relate to.

Henry stoked my interest in fossils, drawing me into his uni-
verse. While most kids outgrow dinosaurs, Henry retained his
love of them and made me feel it was okay to be an adult and still
be thrilled by dinosaurs. In that respect, he gave me "permission"
to continue my infatuation with fossils.

That day in January, while in New York, I broached the idea
of finding my own T. rex. I already knew the obstacles—scarcity
and finding a way into the field. Mounting a dinosaur safari is
not something you embark on casually. You don't just consult
The Yellow Pages or scroll through Google. You have to know an
insider in the paleontology community. That's where Henry
Galiano came in.

We had a good rapport, but I was still nervous about asking
for help. I might come across as a head case. In the art world, it
would have been the equivalent of a novice painter requesting
to hang out with Jasper Johns. After all, a slew of dinosaur hunters had spent their entire lives in vain pursuit of a T. rex. Was I
foolish enough to think I could accomplish what *fewer than three
dozen* hunters in the entire history of paleontology had been able
to achieve?

I blurted out, "Listen Henry, I know this is going to sound a little off-the-wall, but I want to hire you to help me get a T. rex."

"You mean you want to buy one? I know of a superb cast with a complete skull and two—"

"No, you don't understand," I said, cutting him off. "I want to find one."

"Are you serious?"

"Absolutely."

Without hesitation, as if this were an everyday request, Henry said, "Sure, why not? I'd love an excuse to get out in the field this summer. And don't worry about paying me—just cover my expenses."

Then he said, "Oh, there's one other thing. Don't expect to be embraced by the other dinosaur hunters."

"What do you mean?" I asked.

"You have no idea what you're in for," said Henry, suddenly growing restive. "Dinosaur hunters are a secretive group. Digging for vertebrate fossils is competitive. If you think you're going to get these guys to share their collecting sites with you, you're wrong."

"Come on, Henry. I wouldn't expect that to happen."

"You're dealing with fear at every level. Private ranchers are skittish about allowing collectors on their property. It can take years to win their trust. University professors won't share any of their files unless you're also an academic. The toughest group are the fossil dealers themselves. They only care about protecting their livelihood. When they hear you're sniffing around for a T. rex—which puts you in direct competition with them—they're not going to want to have anything to do with you."

I was taken aback. "Yeah, but I'll have *you* in my corner."

Trying to remain patient, Henry said, "You're still missing the point. Even though you're aligned with me, you're not one of *us*. You're asking people who don't know you to take you into their confidence—*this is how they make their living*. With me, it's different—I *know* you."

After a short pause, he said, "Why don't you do this—meet me in Tucson next month?"

I knew he was referring to the Gem, Mineral and Fossil Showcase of Tucson, the unofficial convention of the fossil world.

"I can personally introduce you to some of the major T. rex hunters, but you'll still have to win them over. See what you can learn—whatever they're willing to tell you."

Then, as an afterthought, he added, "There is one guy who might help you out . . . but he's the wackiest of them all."

"Who?"

"Bob Detrich. But he's better known as the Fossil King."

The annual February fair in Tucson boasted the largest number of fossil dealers in one city. Yet the dealers spread themselves throughout hundreds of inexpensive motel rooms. By day, they carefully arrange their specimens on every available surface in their rooms: on beds, dressers, and chairs—even bathtubs. By night, the dealers packed up their treasures and slept in the very beds that only hours earlier served as display cases.

The show's format calls for potential buyers to speed-read each dealer's offerings. Once your eyes lock onto a desirable fossil, then the real fun begins—it's time to bargain.

Collector: "I'll give you $125 for that *Phacops rana* trilobite."

Dealer: "Sorry, the price is a buck-fifty [$150]. I'm sure you're aware that it's from Sylvania—you know, the Medusa shale quarry which happens to be permanently flooded. You're not going to see any more trilobites crawl out of there!"

Collector: "Yeah, but your trilobite is all curled up. It's also missing its glabella. The dealer down the hall has a *Phacops* that's almost a full two inches—perfectly flat—with a *Paraspirifer bownockeri* on the same slab. And he only wants $250 for it!"

Dealer: "So buy it from him!"

Collector: "Alright, forget the trilobite. What about those crinoid stems over there? Those are the biggest blastoids I've ever seen!"

I had arrived in Tucson mid-day with plenty of time to get an overview of the fair. The scuttlebutt was that all the action was at the Vagabond Motel. Pulling into the parking lot, I looked up at a hodgepodge of banners draped over the second floor railing. Some had a wonderful hand-made quality, boasting striking graphics. Others simply advertised the specialty of each dealer: "Ice Age Fossil Ivory!" "Arizona's Finest Petrified Wood!" "New Find—Prehistoric Amber!" "Short Face Bear—Complete Skeleton!"

The motel's corridors were frantic with activity. A small hoard of collectors seemed to jump in and out of rooms in a manner resembling that ridiculous arcade game, Whack-a-Mole. After visiting just five dealers, I was already overwhelmed. There was too much to see. The Vagabond held over sixty rooms (plus the lobby and banquet hall). Multiplying that figure by the eight designated show motels, I realized there were over 480 rooms to check out. Switching tactics, I decided to pursue fossil dealers exclusively, rather than include gems and minerals.

Making the rounds, it dawned on me that few dealers were as intriguing as their fossils. The scene was male-dominated with beer bellies galore. Many dealers were in desperate need of a shave and a shower. Most wore jeans and well-worn plaid shirts. Shoes were either work boots or inexpensive cowboy boots. Overall they were a scruffy lot, but a few dapper merchants sported western shirts with bolo ties, one with a real scorpion encased in the clear plastic clasp.

The scene was quite a contrast from a gathering of art dealers in Basel or Miami where fashion was crucial. I wanted to rush out and look for the first western wear shop I could find. It was time to blend in, whatever it took to cross over to their world.

On the second floor, I found a dealer with a display of Ice Age material worthy of the Page Museum that housed the La Brea Tar Pits specimens in Los Angeles. The highlight was a pair of curved ivory mammoth tusks that measured a good six-feet tall. They were 20,000 years old with a beautiful caramel-brown patina. Each was mounted on its own free-standing black steel base and was positioned just far enough apart to have been anatomically correct, had they been protruding from the mouth of an actual mammoth. Price? $18,000 for the pair. Although importing elephant ivory from Africa and Asia was against the law, possessing fossil ivory wasn't. Most of the ivory was sold to artisans, not collectors. Whether slated for belt buckles, money clips, or earrings, the physical beauty of the ivory was undeniable. The vast majority of tusks were smooth and sensuous to the touch, darkened and weathered by time and several ice ages. A cross-section of prehistoric ivory revealed growth-ring patterns, similar to a tree. Choice fragments were stained by various minerals and often contained flecks of orange and rust.

I was about to leave the room when my eye caught a small placard offering "Genuine Woolly Mammoth Hair." Sure enough, a handful of sandwich-size Ziploc bags held several strands of long reddish-brown hair. For the bargain price of twenty dollars, you could be the proud owner of the remnants of a creature that Cro-Magnon man once stalked.

"That's amazing—actual woolly mammoth fur. Where does it come from?"

"It comes from a mammoth!"

Wincing, I replied, "I mean, where was it found?"

"Oh, probably Siberia. Almost every year a mummified mammoth carcass seems to thaw out of the permafrost. The trick is getting to them before the wild animals do. Believe it or not, they're still edible after thousands of years in the ground. There have even been a few mammoths—or was that mastodons?—found in Alaska."

"So all of this stuff is real?"

By the look on the dealer's face, I sensed I had wounded his pride. I quickly rephrased my question, "Sorry—I know it's real, but it's just so . . . *out there*."

The dealer smiled indulgently.

I'm a collector by nature, but I decided to keep my powder dry. Zipping through a dozen rooms, I found everything from your basic run-of-the-mill Utah trilobites to gift shop quality (read: poorly preserved) Ohio Valley horn corals. Pyritized brachiopods (clams covered with fool's gold) were also in vogue that year.

There was even a room filled with coprolites, also known as dinosaur dung. Coprolites are yellow-brown in color and range from a few inches to about a foot long. As you might guess, their forms are rather tubular and spiraled, as if your dog had squeezed one out about a hundred million years ago. Yet these fossils are a serious matter to paleontologists. By using a jeweler's saw to section a piece, and looking at it under a microscope, you can learn a lot about an extinct creature's diet.

While visions of enormous dinosaurs performing their bodily functions danced in my head, I went searching for Henry Galiano. He was exhibiting vertebrate material that had recently been discovered in China. When I greeted him, he was using a dental tool to gingerly flick away bits of rock surrounding a small fossil bone. After we spent a few minutes catching up, he said, "Want to see what's wrong with this business? There's a Russian down the hall selling doctored trilobites."

I eagerly followed Henry to a room filled with a large array of trilobites, artfully presented on pieces of crushed red velvet. Trilobites were bottom dwelling sea creatures resembling oversize pill bugs. At first glance, they looked right as rain. Each marine invertebrate had well-defined appendages and long protruding antennae that extended skyward. I was duly impressed by how the preparator had preserved the fragile antennae. In fact, I didn't recall ever seeing antennae that stood up vertically, usually they were exposed still embedded in the surrounding matrix.

Under the watchful eye of the Russian dealer, I continued to examine the specimens, carefully searching for signs of fraud.

"I like your trilobites. Would you happen to have a spare magnifying glass handy?"

The Russian shrugged and said, in heavily accented English, "Don't have. Sorry."

"How much are they?"

The dealer grinned broadly and said, "Not worry. I make you good price. How many you buy?"

I glanced at Henry, looking for direction. He motioned me out of the room. Once out of earshot, he said, "Did you notice anything funny about those antennae? Are you ready for this? *They come from an entirely different species of trilobite.* The Russian took them from some other trilobites and superglued them onto the ones we were looking at. They're Frankensteins!"

I said to Henry, "What a crook," while secretly admiring the dealer's ingenuity.

Before I got too infatuated, he said, "Are you ready for the *real* show? Follow me."

CHAPTER TWO

All Hail the Fossil King

enry Galiano led me to a spacious room occupied by some of the biggest dealers in the fossil business including Triebold Paleontology. The centerpiece of Triebold's display was a twenty-four-foot long Edmontosaurus (Duckbill) that had been cast from a truly exceptional specimen. This skeleton revealed scars from an attack by a meat-eater—deep gashes from serrated-edge teeth were clearly visible on a section of the lower jaw. It appeared the predator had grabbed the plant-eater by the throat, didn't have a firm enough grip, and it got away. There were calcium deposits around the wounds, indicating the injury had healed and the creature had survived.

As I admired the beast, Mike Triebold came over and introduced himself by cutting straight to the chase. "Henry tells me the two of you are planning to search for a T. rex!"

Triebold appeared to be in his late forties. Of average height, he sported a full head of blond hair and a meticulously trimmed beard—almost too well-groomed to be a paleontologist. He was dressed in khakis and a matching vest bearing the name of his company. While looking over his inventory, we talked about the economics of the fossil business.

"Without prying, how much can someone make working for a fossil company—can you make $5,000 a month?"

"That's prying," said Triebold, good-naturedly.

He then offered a revealing glimpse into the precarious life of a commercial fossil dealer: "I employ twenty-two people, pay them a salary, offer a health plan, pay worker's comp—you name it. The whole idea is to keep the place running—not so much to make a profit—but to keep everyone employed. I have good people who are highly skilled so I don't want to lose them. There have to be enough projects—specimens to prepare, mounts to build—that sort of thing."

Triebold spoke with great passion. All he was trying to do was keep his team intact until he landed the big one. Then he suddenly brightened.

"I don't know if Henry told you, but we're currently excavating the most complete juvenile T. rex ever found—we've named it 'Sir William' and he's a beauty!"

"A juvenile? Will it be for sale?" I asked.

"Why do you want to know?"

"Just curious."

Triebold paused for a moment, deciding whether to respond.

"Once it's out of the ground and mounted, I'm planning to ask $3.5 million for it," he said, without flinching.

At first, I was a little surprised by his steep price. But Triebold seemed confident that he'd find a buyer. I asked, "How do you negotiate the price of a dinosaur? Let's say, hypothetically, I offered you only $3 million. Would you take it?"

Triebold looked a bit nonplussed and I hoped I hadn't offended him.

"Well, I guess I would certainly listen if someone made me an offer. But what's not negotiable is that I won't sell it to a private individual—it has to go to a museum. Now that's not saying that I won't sell to an individual who will eventually donate it to a museum."

While he was telling me this, I sensed there was more to his story. He didn't entirely trust me. When it came to the fossil biz, I was learning that Henry Galiano could get me in the front door, but I'd have to negotiate my own seat at the dinner table.

Triebold continued, "You may not know this, but I've been constructing a dinosaur museum in Colorado, which will open to the public this summer. Give me your address and I'll invite you to the opening. Should be a great party."

Just then, I heard someone come up behind me. I twisted around in my chair and was greeted by a tall lanky guy with a firm handshake and an over-solicitous smile. I glanced over at Henry, who raised his eyebrows in mock incredulity. Then it hit me. The "show" he spoke of was about to begin.

"Howdy, I'm Bob Detrich."

Bob handed me a business card which featured a line drawing of a T. rex wearing a crown. Above it was the name Robert Detrich and the title, "The Fossil King." He was based in Kansas, the home of the famous "Niobrara Formation," an ancient ocean bed whose chalk deposits often yielded the fearsome Mosasaur—the fish-like T. rex of the high seas. At the bottom of the card were the words: "Best in the World."

Pointing to these words, I asked, "What exactly does this mean?"

"It means I offer the best fossils in the world!"

Why, I wondered, was Triebold rolling his eyes?

At my suggestion, Bob pulled up a chair, while Triebold and I continued to talk about the fossil market. Although I tried to coax Bob into the conversation, he remained silent. All of a sudden, he leapt up from his seat and exclaimed, "I'll be right back—there's something you need to see."

A few minutes later, Bob returned holding a small open cardboard tray that fossil and mineral dealers refer to as a "flat."

"Here," was all Bob said, as he casually handed it to me.

Still seated, I peered down into the flat and saw approximately fifteen unimpressive stone fragments. The largest one measured two inches across, the smallest perhaps half an inch. Each piece was greenish-gray, had a sandy texture, and was mottled with a few specks of black and dull yellow. I held up the biggest piece, carefully examining it. To the untrained eye, it appeared to be utterly worthless. There was no obvious form to it. All I saw was a faint impression on one side that resembled the skin of a reptile. I knew there were several documented finds of skin impressions that came from Duckbills, but never from a carnivore.

I made eye contact with Bob. "Dinosaur skin?"

With a gleam in his eyes Bob said, "Not just any dinosaur—you're holding the first known skin impressions from a Tyrannosaurus rex!"

I looked over at Triebold who continued to smile. I was shocked. How could this be? What proof did he have?

Bob went on, "These pieces were found within a few inches of a T. rex bone that I uncovered—they couldn't possibly be anything else."

"If that's true . . ." my voice trailed off.

"You got it—it's the Holy Grail of dinosaurs!"

After I recovered my surprise, I asked the obvious question, "What has the paleontology community said about this? Do they agree with you?"

Bob sighed. "Well, they're dubious."

"Assuming you're correct, this material must be worth a fortune. Not to be crass, but are these fragments for sale?"

"They sure are. I've priced them at $8,000 a gram or $1 million for the group."

I thought about it. If these were really the first known impressions of T. rex skin, they were easily worth whatever he wanted for them. But without conclusive proof, I wasn't quite sure how he hoped to convince someone to pay his price. Regardless, I wanted to believe they were genuine. It was too delicious to think otherwise.

Henry turned to me. "Listen, Richard, I've got to get back to my room for a few appointments today."

"Right," I said. "Catch you later."

The moment Henry left, Bob ran after me and said, "I didn't want to say anything while I was in Mike's booth, but I have some other great things for sale. Why don't you come with me next door to the Co-Op?"

With nothing to lose, I followed him to the Fossil Co-Op. Once inside the modern warehouse, Bob pointed out the various highlights, including a vast display of infamous Moroccan fossils. *The New York Times Sunday Magazine* had recently done an exposé on the subject, titled, "The Fossil Frenzy." Its subhead read, "Trilobites have become the latest thing rich Americans collect. To feed the demand, enterprising Moroccans are dedicating themselves to a life of fossil digging—and fakery."

Just then, a collector approached Bob. After some hushed talk, he turned to me, "Why don't you check out some of the other dealers—I need to speak to this gentleman. Meet me over at my brother's space when you're done and I'll show you some things that'll blow your mind. Oh, and make sure you see the Megalodon Man."

The *Megalodon Man?* He sounded like some sort of comic book superhero. His real name turned out to be Vito Bertucci. Over fifty, he had long black hair, shot full of silver, that peeked out from under a watchman's cap. His grubby sweatshirt, draped over an ample paunch, was stenciled with a gargantuan Megalodon shark jaw. Around his neck dangled a gold chain with—what else?—a lone fossil shark tooth.

One of the most desirable of all fossils is the six-inch-long tooth of the *Carcharodon Megalodon*—a school bus-sized ancestor of today's great white shark with jaws large enough for a man to stand inside its mouth. Not only are Megalodon teeth lengthy, they are also heavy. They have a pleasing physicality to them when you cradle one in your hand. In that respect, they are unlike any fossil I have ever held.

Despite the fact that the average shark shed approximately 12,000 teeth during a lifetime, relatively few Megalodon teeth have been found—even fewer in good condition. Teeth with true aesthetic beauty are extremely expensive, at least by fossil market standards.

Marveling at two display cases crammed with immense fossil shark teeth, I said, "Nice teeth—better than the ones I saw yesterday at the Vagabond."

"The Vagabond? Any major Megalodon teeth you see at the show passed through my hands at some point. I'm the godfather of the fossil shark tooth business."

"See that one over there?" he continued. "That's almost *seven* inches—turned down $15,000 for it. It's one of the ten largest teeth ever found. Now look at this case over here. Have you ever seen so many large teeth in this condition? I just sold the whole collection for $200,000. That may sound like a lot of money—but it's not!"

Bertucci went on, "You have to realize I spent thirty years of my life diving to find them in the Cooper River [South Carolina]. And believe me, the water's freezing—you don't want to go down there unless you know what you're doing. The currents are dangerous and you can easily drown.* Plus, you dive down from thirty to seventy feet and it's so dark on the bottom that all you can do is feel around for the teeth. You find them by touch."

Helping himself to a Krispy Kreme donut, the Megalodon Man stared at me and asked, "Are you looking for shark teeth?"

---

* Eight months later (in October 2004) Bertucci actually did drown while searching for shark teeth. Apparently, he was so worried about revealing the location of his favorite hunting spot, that he disregarded the cardinal rule of diving—never dive alone.

"No. I'm actually putting together an expedition to search for a T. rex."

"No shit."

I continued, "Hey, maybe you could be of some help—you seem to be connected. Any chance of introducing me to someone you know who hunts for T. rexes?"

Ignoring my question, he said, "I really hate to see my collection go. But the business is changing. Nowadays, when you go diving you only find one or two teeth a day. In the old days—the early 1980s—you would often scoop up a hundred teeth a day."

"What changed?"

"I'll tell you what changed," he said with disgust. "People started selling on eBay and mentioned all the rivers where you could find them."

"Why would they do that?"

"Because when you buy fossils the details surrounding the site where the fossil was discovered are everything. People demand to know the locality of the fossil so they can date it, identify the species—that's how it works. So now, thanks to eBay, the cat's out of the bag. Instead of three guys with 1,000 Megalodon teeth, you now have 1,000 guys with three teeth."

In the age of the Internet, information could expand a collector's knowledge and enjoyment, but it also destroys the dealer's advantage. If dealers can't make a living, then they can't do exhibitions and catalogs, which expand the parameters of the field. Now, eBay was making it so easy to sell things, that the market was being flooded with merchandise, resulting in depressed prices.

My next stop at the Fossil Co-Op was the Green River Stone Company. Founded by Tom Lindgren, an athletic-looking fellow in his fifties, the company specialized in presenting fossils as natural works of art. Years ago, Lindgren bought a quarry in Wyoming called Fossil Lake, known primarily for its abundance of fossil fish. There are also plenty of turtles, crocodiles, and palm fronds embedded in stone. The fossils are often a pleasing burnt umber, which contrasts beautifully with the sheets of gray and beige-colored shale in which they're found. They're sold as art.

What also sets the Green River Stone Company's fossils apart is the way the specimens are prepared. At the quarry, fossils are detected by their outline, even though they are still covered by a thin layer of calcium carbonate. Once a fossil-bearing sheet of rock is removed from the quarry, it's taken back to a preparation lab. At that point, Lindgren makes an aesthetic decision. The idea is to treat each section like an artist's canvas. You don't want a slab where the fossil fish is displayed smack-dab in the middle. Instead, you're looking for a sheet that can be cut so a fish appears slightly off center, often surrounded by smaller complimentary fish.

Once the composition is determined, the preparator gradually removes the calcium carbonate to reveal the underlying fossil. The slab is cut to a crisp rectilinear shape and tastefully framed, just like an oil painting. "Most of what you see here is in the $7,500 to $30,000 range. But if you want to get into something spectacular like that major pair of palm fronds over there, then you're looking at big money—$240,000 to be exact."

Impressed with the price, I walked over for a closer examination of his most expensive fossils on display. What was astonishing was how the 9' x 5' slabs corresponded to one another. A single sheet of stone had been perfectly split down the middle, creating mirror images of the palm fronds. But what really caught my eye was the way the surrounding rock had been intentionally layered. By gently stripping away wafer-thin sections, the preparator was able to create wonderful illusions of depth.

Lindgren said, "People like having my fossils in their homes. They're calming; they take us back to our roots. You find yourself becoming part of the piece."

He was right. The more I stared at a fossil "painting," the more I lost myself in the natural compositions of fish and the occasional sting ray. It *was* analogous to viewing great art. When you look at a painting, you want to feel the presence of the artist in the room with you. In this case, you wanted to feel as if the extinct creatures had come back to life—which was exactly what it felt like at that moment.

A few weeks after the Tucson Fossil Fair I checked in with Henry Galiano at his Manhattan shop. "By the way, are we making any progress on our T. rex expedition? I'd sure feel a lot better if I knew we had a definite plan to get out in the field."

Henry responded cordially. "You probably didn't know this, but when 'Sue' was found, there were also a few rex bones from other individuals—there may have been a family of T. rexes at Maurice Williams's ranch. I wasn't going to tell you until I knew for certain, but what I'm planning to do is call Maurice to see if he'll let us come out."

Maurice Williams. The name hit me like a sledgehammer.

CHAPTER THREE

The Legacy of Sue

Whenever a fossil dealer hears the name Maurice Williams, he either wants to propose a toast or leave the room in disgust. Everyone has an opinion. To the uninitiated, Maurice Williams is the man who turned the fossil business on its head. After all, the dinosaur named "Sue" was found on his land. It was also his subsequent lawsuit that led to unwanted fame for Susan Hendrickson, jail time for Peter Larson, and vast riches for Williams.

The story of Sue, the subject of countless articles and two books, is indeed remarkable and remains relevant. It unfolded back in 1990, when Peter Larson and his crew were searching the badlands of his native South Dakota for dinosaur bones. He had been following his boyhood dream of some day owning his own dinosaur museum. Larson had found his first fossil at age four and went on to make fossil hunting his life's work. As he put it, "Rather than play cowboys and Indians, I played curator."

Larson, his brother Neal, and a partner went on to form the Black Hills Institute of Geological Research, in Hill City, South Dakota, which supplied fossils and casts to museums, universities, and collectors. The Institute's shop, "Everything Prehistoric," handled dino-related books, jewelry, and children's toys. While not terribly lucrative, the money earned from this venture allowed Larson to pursue his collecting goals. Despite having had great success at finding dinosaurs, especially Duckbills, the dinosaur that he wanted most still eluded him—a T. rex.

Before Larson started his search, he had approached Maurice Williams, a member of the Cheyenne River Sioux, who owned many acres of prime fossil-yielding badlands near Buffalo, South Dakota. Larson had reason to believe that dinosaurs could be found on Williams's land. Permission was granted to search for them. Chances were that Williams was charmed by the thought of dinosaurs buried on his ranch. Larson explained to Williams that if they found anything worthwhile, he would pay him something for it. But then Larson hedged his bet by explaining they didn't have much money, so not to expect a windfall.

Although the general public knows what a dinosaur is, thanks to the film industry most people have an overly romantic vision of paleontology, like the sanitized version presented in *Jurassic Park*. They've been led to believe that it's a world of crisp safari clothing and spacious clean tents, where the valiant hunter experiences a daily (or at least weekly) series of triumphant discoveries. Having dug for fossils, I can vouch that it is hard, dirty work. You dig until your hand grows numb from gripping a rock hammer and your vision goes blurry from staring at the ground for hours on end. There are few creature comforts out in the field (try going a week without a shower) and even fewer moments of glory.

Unearthing fossils requires plenty of luck and intuition. But mainly it requires perseverance. Knowing where to look is mandatory. Fossils are only found in sedimentary rock laid down primarily during the Jurassic through Cretaceous periods (approximately 65-205 million years ago). Every state in America contains fossils. But if you're after dinosaurs, your likely target area includes Colorado, Utah, Wyoming, Montana, and South Dakota.

Only specific conditions allowed prehistoric life to be preserved. For openers, an animal had to die and be buried quickly, preventing bone-decaying oxygen from seeping in. Let's say a Stegosaurus expired on the banks of a river bed and was immediately covered with mud. Let's also say that over eons of time the beast continued to be covered with multiple layers of silt. Assuming that the right combination of minerals were in the ground, they would eventually seep into the bones and gradually replace their structure, ultimately turning bone to stone.

But that's just the first step. The end game occurs when, after millions of years of geologic upheaval, the layer of rock where the animal was buried eventually pushes up to the surface. Through erosion the fossil may finally become visible, but it's also subject to the very elements that exposed it: wind, rain, frost, snow, and sand storms will destroy it. If the fossil isn't discovered within a few years, you can pretty much kiss it good-bye.

The best-case scenario occurs when a fossil hunter sees only the smallest exposed piece of bone sticking out from a cliff. If the stars are aligned, that same bone may lead to finding the preserved dinosaur. Even then, most dinosaurs died from being attacked, so their bones may have been scattered or carried off by scavengers.

The vast majority of dinosaurs found were plant eaters, such as the ever-famous Brontosaurus (now called Apatosaurus), Stego-saurus, and Triceratops. The fierce meat-eaters were much rarer. It's analogous to today's animal kingdom where there are far fewer dominant predators, such as tigers and lions, than wildebeest and zebras. So it follows that the king of carnivores, Tyrannosaurus rex, was relatively rare to begin with. What's more, not only are T. rexes hard to find, they are never found complete. Up until the discovery of Sue, the finest specimen in existence was only fifty percent original bone.

Peter Larson was aware of the tremendous odds against finding a T. rex, having searched for over two decades and still coming up empty-handed. Yet, he never lost his focus, desperately hoping to find one and make it the centerpiece of his planned museum. With one magnificent T. rex—one dinosaur with star power—his museum would become world famous.

On August 12, 1990, Larson was out in the field, probing a promising outcrop. Having detected evidence of bone, he went back to his jeep for tools. That's when he noticed one of its tires was almost flat. After determining that his spare was useless, he decided to catch a ride back into town to have both tires repaired. Before leaving, Larson called his colleague, Susan Hendrickson, over and explained that he'd be back soon.

Hendrickson was a professional adventurer. Her credits included such disparate ventures as dealing fossil amber and harvesting lobsters. With her ready smile, long blond hair, and upbeat personality, she was a welcome presence in the field. At the time, she was romantically linked to Larson, but that was winding down and their relationship had apparently evolved into a professional collaboration.

While Larson was gone, Hendrickson was lured (or so she said) by some mysterious force that told her to explore a certain exposed cliff. Sure enough, she looked up, and there, about seven feet above the ground, was a ribbon of articulated dinosaur vertebrae protruding from the side of the rock face.

When Larson returned, he saw what Hendrickson had found. Small pieces of bone that had weathered out and fallen from the cliff. He picked one up to study it. He saw that the internal structure of the bone was honey-combed. The technical term was *camellate*, meaning the interior was composed of large hollow capillaries. This, combined with a few other indicators could only mean one thing. It was a large dinosaur. It was a theropod (carnivorous). And it was a Tyrannosaurus rex. As he shared his conclusion with Hendrickson, he was overwhelmed by the potential magnitude of what stood before him.

Larson named the dinosaur Sue, instantly immortalizing Susan Hendrickson. Ever humble, Hendrickson returned the compliment by telling Larson that the dinosaur was his. She was "giving" it to him. Larson instinctively knew what he had to do next—secure the dinosaur by acquiring the rights to it from the landowner. This is where the story got complicated.

On the fateful day Sue was found, Larson called Williams with news of the discovery. Telling him they had uncovered something pretty good, Larson offered Williams $5,000. Probably thinking that it was found money, Williams readily accepted. While in retrospect this may have seemed a paltry offer, it was actually within some reason. According to Larson, $5,000 was a record for a skeleton still in the ground.

To put this figure into perspective, it is important to know that excavating a dinosaur is extremely expensive. The cost of carefully removing a large skeleton, packing it, shipping it, preparing it, and mounting it can easily run hundreds of thousands of dollars—or more. Regardless, no one but Larson and Williams will ever know the exact language of the bargain that was struck that day.

What happened next was that Larson, assuming he owned Sue, began excavating her. As the dinosaur came to light, he must have been beside himself with joy. The skeleton was almost ninety percent complete. It was also becoming clear that it was the *largest and best-preserved* Tyrannosaurus rex ever discovered. Not only was he going to have a dinosaur for his museum, he was going to have the quintessential dinosaur. Sue's charisma was readily apparent. In fact, in the history of American paleontology, there was no precedent for Sue. No dinosaur would ever go on to receive this much attention.

Before long, local reporters heard about the discovery, and word went out that something extraordinary was going on at the Williams ranch. Eventually, the story reached the Sioux tribal council. Showing greater savvy than Williams, they quickly surmised that the rex was worth quite a bit more than $5,000. There was also mounting pressure from Williams's family who sensed he should have received more money. As Larson got wind of these rumblings, he worked overtime to get Sue out of the ground, completing the task in a little over two weeks.

By now, the tribal council had called in attorneys who informed them that Williams may have owned the land, but the Sioux people held final jurisdiction over it. The tribal council concluded that the dinosaur was not Williams's to sell. It was theirs. At that point, Larson knew there was a problem but decided to wait it out, hoping the situation would dissipate. It didn't.

Things got messier after Williams went public to deny that he had sold Larson the dinosaur for $5,000—*of course he knew it was worth more than that*. He claimed all Larson's money bought was "the right to excavate it" (whatever that meant). Before Sue was barely out of the ground, her legacy had already come down to money. Or as Williams succinctly put it, "It always comes down to money."

The controversy reached a stage where Larson needed legal help. Patrick Duffy, a slick cigar-smoking attorney, was hired to defend Larson and make sure he was allowed to hang on to Sue. In a preliminary hearing it was determined that although Williams did indeed own the land, it was being held for him in trust by the United States government (for tax advantages). This meant that Sue was now a federal matter.

Not long after the ruling, all hell broke loose. Early one morning, a busload of National Guard troops, accompanied by federal agents, descended on the tiny town of Hill City, South Dakota (population 650). They began unfurling "Sheriff's Line—Do Not Cross" yellow plastic tape around Larson's Black Hills Institute and made preparations to confiscate Sue. Predictably, the media had been tipped off. Sensational photos of the National Guard carting away Sue were picked up by the Associated Press. Almost overnight, the story of Sue's incarceration had become national news. A video was shot of the townspeople rallying around the T. rex, trying to prevent the National Guard from taking her away.

Tears were shed and protest signs were displayed but none of it did any good.

Larson and his family were outraged, but apparently not half as outraged as the federal government. They essentially wanted Larson to surrender all claims to Sue. On the surface this seemed absurd. Larson had received permission from the landowner to search his property, found the dinosaur, and bought it fair and square (even if he underpaid for it). But there was a more ominous side to the story.

The government was using the threat of a trial to pursue Larson on other charges. For one thing, they were investigating him for taking more than $10,000 in cash out of the country, on a fossil buying trip, without declaring it. That was a felony. There was also the matter of a fossil catfish, which had been poached from federal lands by a "collector," who in turn sold it to Larson. That meant Larson was in violation of the Federal Antiquities Act. Another felony. While the government was at it, they also charged Peter's brother, Neal Larson, and a partner in the Black Hills Institute with related crimes.

The government indicated that if Peter Larson dropped his claim to Sue, they would let him off with a slap on the wrist on the other two charges—money-laundering and violating the Federal Antiquities Act. Though both of these charges usually resulted in fines, jail sentences were a possibility. Whether it was emotional attachment or his attorney's advice (or a combination of the two), Larson decided not to relinquish his claim to Sue. The case went to trial, while Larson went through tremendous mental anguish to say nothing of ruinous expense.

For a while it looked good. But Duffy got a little cocky with the press, which didn't sit well with the prosecutor. While Duffy pleaded for leniency in the form of probation, the prosecutor demanded three years of prison time. Despite a plethora of supportive letters written on Larson's behalf, the judge was not moved. He found Peter Larson guilty and sentenced him to two years in jail. Neal Larson and the partner were acquitted. Compounding Peter Larson's defeat, Maurice Williams was declared the sole legal owner of the prize T. rex. The judge determined that Sue was part of the land (like timber or oil deposits) and thus was Williams's property.

In 1997, after Sue had been in storage for seven years, Williams decided to put her up for auction at Sotheby's. The auction house titled the sale, "Tyrannosaurus rex—A Highly Important and Virtually Complete Skeleton." An elaborate sales catalog offered impressive photos and scientific data on the dinosaur. Once you finished reading it, there was no doubt in your mind that whatever the rex finally sold for, it wouldn't be enough. Since this was an unprecedented sale, Sotheby's had been uncertain where to place the pre-sale estimate. After consulting with Henry Galiano, they decided to go with a nice round figure that was sure to stir up plenty of publicity: $1 million.

You can imagine how upset Larson must have been when he learned about the sale. He still held out faint hope that he could buy her back privately. But now it was going to auction. At that point, he had already served his jail time but couldn't fly to New York because he was on probation and under home confinement. Still, he somehow managed to put together a syndicate to try to reacquire Sue. Armed with a war chest of a little over $1 million, provided by a wealthy local businessman, Larson sent his benefactor to New York to bid on what he thought was rightfully his. He was still cautiously optimistic that Sue would belong to him again.

At the actual sale, the bidding opened at $500,000 and sprinted to $1 million so quickly that Larson's representative never had a chance to raise his paddle. Once the bidding reached $1.5 million, Larson's agent exceeded his limit and got off his one and only bid. However, it proved a lost cause as the bidding quickly passed the $5 million threshold. At that point, Chicago's Field

Museum of Natural History jumped into the fray. Backed by Disney and McDonald's, they rode the bidding all the way to its final hammer price of $7.6 million. When the buyer's premium was added, the full selling price came to $8.3 million. After sixty-five million years in the ground, Sue's final resting place was determined in a matter of minutes.

Since Williams's land was held in government trust, he walked away with approximately $7.6 million—tax-free. Yet, despite his incredible good fortune, he still harbored deep animosity toward Larson. According to Henry Galiano, he also refused a number of museum-affiliated paleontologists' requests to see what else was on his land, even though there was evidence of other rexes. The tantalizing possibility of finding another Sue on the Williams ranch was rapidly becoming the ultimate dinosaur tease.

Now, Henry was proposing that we meet up with Maurice Williams to find a T. rex of our own.

CHAPTER FOUR

Meeting Maurice Williams

S taring at Henry, slightly in awe, I asked, "Why would Maurice Williams let us on his property to collect when it's been off limits to everyone else?"

"You're forgetting something," responded Henry. "When he consigned Sue to Sotheby's, I was hired not only as a consultant, but as a liaison between the auction house and Maurice. Over time we got to be friends—I'm the only one he trusts in the dinosaur market."

Back when Sotheby's David Redden had flown to the Williams ranch to secure the consignment, he contacted Henry to serve as a "paleontology adviser." Henry had been recommended to Sotheby's by the American Museum of Natural History in New York. Once Redden had interviewed him and was satisfied that he knew his stuff, he was hired on the spot. Henry agreed to be paid a flat fee, rather than a percentage of the sale, and had to sign a contract which included a confidentiality agreement. At that point, Redden outlined his strategy for selling the rex.

David Redden was known around Sotheby's for coming up with incredible stuff, often material never seen before at auction. His past triumphs included a sale of Russian space history, including cosmonaut uniforms and moon rocks. He also put together a sale of one of the few surviving copies of the Declaration of Independence, found by some fortunate soul in the back of an old frame bought at a flea market. A more recent Redden coup was the auction of the world's rarest coin, the 1933 gold Double Eagle (a twenty-dollar gold piece) for $7.6 million.

When Redden set his sights on Sue, he said, "I wanted to make sure two things happened. First, that Maurice Williams got the right price. And second, that Sue got the right home. To that end, we made it clear that American institutional buyers be given the advantage of having three years to pay for her."

But as Henry remembered, "Nobody had ever seen or sold a dinosaur like Sue before. It was difficult to put a price tag on her because there was nothing to compare her to. Dinosaurs weren't exactly a known commodity at auction. My initial estimate was $500,000—but that was just a guess. David Redden came up with the million-dollar estimate. He felt Sue was the best of its kind and, since he was used to dealing with 'the best of its kind' in many categories, he had a sense that it was worth at least a million dollars. You have to realize that we were selling a T. rex that was still in its plaster jackets (to protect the bones when they were moved from the field). I told Redden that whoever bought it would have to spend an additional $2.5 million to properly prepare and mount it. Preparing a major dinosaur can take 25,000 hours of skilled labor—and that doesn't include mounting."

Henry continued, "But I also told Sotheby's that even if someone spent a total of $3 million, Sue's value as a public draw was immeasurable. Without patting myself on the back, I was right about that. Just ask the Field Museum."

"Maurice must have been pretty excited when he heard about that million-dollar estimate."

"Not really," said Henry. "Maurice was a rather successful rancher who was used to participating in cattle and horse auctions. In a certain way, this wasn't that much different."

"So you're saying the money wasn't that important to him?"

"Not as important as his self-esteem—he didn't want to be taken for a sap. For him, the sale was mostly about justice."

"Well, let me ask you this. Did you do anything else besides appraise Sue?"

"Sure. I was involved with every phase of the auction. Right after I signed my contract, I flew with Redden to the South Dakota School of Mines, where Sue had been stored. We flew there in total secrecy."

"Why was that?"

"Because we didn't want to stir things up with the local press. Since the T. rex was held in trust for Maurice, it was a federal matter. The FBI met us there and kept an eye on us and filmed everything we did. This was pre-9/11—the government had plenty of time on its hands. Basically, we inspected the skeleton and made sure it was packed properly for its trip to New York. That's when I met Maurice for the first time."

"What was your initial impression of him?"

"He was very cool—very business-like. We really didn't get a chance to talk much."

Once they flew back East, Henry met the truck at the other end. The crates containing the bones were placed in a temperature-controlled room. "Sotheby's was extremely cautious about everything. Even if a crate had to be moved only two or three feet, they would call me to come over and supervise. I'm not exaggerating. They were very concerned about their image with all the parties involved: the paleontology community, the government, their clientele, and the general public. But as you know," said Henry, "everything worked out even better than we hoped."

"Well, it sounds like Maurice really owes you for shepherding him through the auction maze," I said.

"Yeah, I guess he does," said Henry. "Don't worry, I'll call him this morning."

Later that day, I caught up with Henry, who was busy negotiating the sale of a prehistoric hyena skull.

"Hi, Richard. Guess who I just spoke with?"

"You got hold of Maurice?"

"We're all set. I told him all about you and he said, 'Any friend of yours . . .' So, I told him we'd probably come out in early June—definitely by the end of the month."

"Sounds like a plan." I was elated.

A few days later, the fair closed and I headed home to San Francisco, secure in the knowledge the hunt was on. I was on my way to becoming a Bonehead.

April blended into May, but still no word from Henry. I grew anxious waiting for him to call. I kept telling myself to play it cool. But impatience got the better of me and I soon found myself dialing him.

"Hello, Maxilla & Mandible," answered a woman's voice that I recognized as Henry's wife.

"Hi Debbie, it's Richard Polsky. May I speak with Henry, please?"

"Just a sec—I'm showing a customer some raccoon penis bones—business as usual," she said with a laugh.

I thought, *What a window into their world.* Thirty seconds and a dozen purchased bones later, Henry got on the phone.

Trying to stay positive and go with the "assumptive close," I said, "Hi buddy, I just wanted to tell you how psyched I am for our trip! Where do you think we should stay in South Dakota? Should I go ahead and make some reservations?"

There was silence at Maxilla & Mandible.

Finally, after a pregnant pause, Henry spoke. "I was going to call you—something's come up."

My heart sank.

"Here's what happened. I recently put in a bid to construct a major exhibit for a museum, and I'm still waiting to hear if I get the job. If I do, then I won't be free until the end of the summer. Unfortunately, I was supposed to know by now. But I just heard the museum's still reviewing proposals and won't make a decision for another three months. Until they send me a signal, I've got to hold off making any plans. Sorry I can't give you more of a commitment—it's just one of those things."

"Wow, yeah," I mumbled.

Sensing my disappointment, he said, "Maybe we could go in late August, although it'll be pretty hot in the badlands. The beginning of the summer's definitely a better time to be out there."

I didn't know what to say. Even if Henry could help me line up an alternative trip, it wouldn't be the same. I was looking forward to being out in the field with *him*. After all, camaraderie is half the fun of the search. But perhaps I could go it alone?

As if reading my mind, Henry said, "What if you went as planned in June? I'll explain what happened to Maurice and try to convince him to let you come out."

Now we were getting somewhere. Grateful that Henry wasn't totally deserting me, I said, "Sounds like I'm going collecting after all."

Henry jumped in, "Wait a minute—not so fast! You don't know who you're dealing with. This is an ornery older guy, who despite receiving a lot of money, went through a big lawsuit and is leery of everyone in the fossil world—except me. Maurice also has a serious distrust of the 'white man.' And then there's his wife . . ."

"I understand," I said. "Look, get me an audience with him and I'll take it from there."

"No problem," said Henry. "Anyway, didn't you say Mike Triebold invited you to the cocktail party for his museum opening? You should go. Who knows? Maybe you'll meet someone you can hire to take you hunting."

Trying to sound gracious, I said, "Thanks, Henry. Go ahead and give Williams a call and let me know what he says."

The next morning, Henry phoned. "Maurice said he's willing to talk to you!"

I responded, "*Talk to me?* Listen, not to sound like an ingrate, but the idea was for me to do some collecting."

Henry started laughing. "You just don't give up, do you? Without me there it's not going to happen. Just speak to him and see if he'll get together with you."

"Fine, I'll do that. But if we hit it off, and I head up to South Dakota, I'm also going to try and see Peter Larson."

"Good idea. But if you call Peter, whatever you do, don't mention Maurice. Likewise, if you talk to Maurice, don't tell him you know Peter. These guys really dislike each other intensely."

"It just hit me," I cracked. "You had a Sioux sue over Sue."

Henry wasn't laughing. Then I added, "Don't worry, I won't push any buttons. It's not a big deal."

"It's a bigger deal than you think. Did you know what happened after the Sue settlement? I heard Maurice ran into Peter in a local restaurant and went up to him and punched him!"

"Get out of here!"

"That's what I heard. Supposedly, Peter hired a lawyer and was going to sue for assault, but never filed the paperwork."

Fascinated, I asked, "What's Maurice's side of the story?"

"He claims all he did was go up to Peter from behind and tap him on the shoulder," said Henry.

"Geez, the two of them are wilder than I thought. Anyway, I'll keep you in the loop and let you know what happens. If I get lucky and convince Peter to take me collecting, I probably won't even go see Maurice—he sounds difficult."

Henry said, "He's a good guy—so is Peter. It's just that you're dealing with people who feel they were burned. I think at this point, they each just want to get on with their lives."

Mindful of Henry's comments, I felt my best approach with Larson was spontaneity. I'd gamble that by just showing up at the Black Hills Institute, I could convince him to take me collecting. I was perfectly willing to pay him for his time. As for Williams, I intuitively knew that making a formal appointment to see him was in order. Though I felt intimidated, there was no avoiding that call.

Maurice Williams's phone rang ten times. I almost felt relieved that he didn't appear to be home. I was just about to give up when a female voice answered.

"Hello."

"Hi. My name is Richard Polsky—I'm a friend of Henry Galiano's. May I speak with Mr. Williams please?"

"What did you say your name was?"

"Richard Polsky."

"I don't know who that is."

"I know *you* don't," I said. "But I'm calling for Mr. Williams."

"Hold on."

Then I heard in the background: "Maurice!" She pronounced it Morris. "There's someone who wants to speak with you!"

"Find out who it is."

The woman returned to the phone and said, "He wants to know who's calling."

I took a deep breath and said, "Please tell him I'm a friend of Henry's. You know—Henry—the dinosaur guy."

"Oh. Hey, Maurice—it's Henry."

Before I could correct her, I heard Maurice hustle over to the phone, pick it up and shout, "Henry? How the hell are you?"

"Hi," I said. "It's *not* Henry. My name's Richard, but I *am* a friend of Henry's. Didn't he tell you about me?"

"No. Who did you say you were?"

Growing exasperated, I said, "Listen, Mr. Williams. Do you remember receiving a recent call from Henry Galiano telling you about a guy who wanted to find a T. rex? Henry told me that you were open to getting together and sharing your experiences."

Before Maurice could answer, I heard a woman's voice in the

background yell, "What does he want?"

Maurice covered the phone—but I could still hear—and yelled back, "The guy's looking for dinosaurs."

"Don't talk to him," said the female voice. "Haven't you had enough?"

Maurice answered, "It's okay. He's a friend of Henry's."

The woman persisted. "He sounds like trouble. I still wouldn't talk to him."

Maurice got back on the phone and said, "It's alright. My wife's just a little protective. What did you want to talk to me about?"

Recovering a bit of my nerve, I said, "Here's the deal, Mr. Williams. I was hoping I could meet with you and hear first-hand about what happened with Sue. I know the story's been told before, but it always seems to be told from the other side's point of view. I'd really like to hear your side of the story."

Maurice perked up and said, "Well, that would be refreshing. When did you want to come see me?"

"I'm planning to come to Hill City in early June. How about if I give you a call right before I take off for my trip?"

"Hill City? You're not planning to talk to that guy down the street are you?" he asked, suddenly growing hostile.

Thinking fast, I said, "Do you mean Peter Larson? I've only met him once. It's your story that I'm interested in."

I don't know how convincing I sounded, but Maurice calmed down.

"Why don't you call back when you're in town, and we'll set something up."

CHAPTER FIVE
Beginnings of Fossil Fever

Now that the expedition had been salvaged, I began to reflect on my keen interest in fossils and how it must have run in my genes. How else could I explain everything my grandfather, Hugo Stern, went through to bring his favorite fossil to America?

Back in 1940, while trying to escape Nazi Germany with his family, he was fortunate enough to book passage on the last ship allowed to leave the country. While most people brought photo albums, clothing, and other bare necessities, my grandfather brought with him a cherished ammonite (the ancestor of the chambered nautilus), a circular stone that must have weighed ten pounds.

The fossil survived the long voyage intact, slipped through the inspection at Ellis Island undisturbed, and eventually landed on an end table in my grandfather's apartment on West 175th Street in New York. In those days, it was common for a family's in-laws to live with them. In my grandfather's case, his mother-in-law wound up under the same roof. Although by most descriptions she was unpleasant, she did contribute to the family's welfare by doing much of the cooking.

One day, she decided to make sauerkraut. Her recipe called for cabbage that had to be carefully crushed to just the right consistency. Failing to find the appropriate kitchen implement, she came upon a curious round stone with a flat-bottom and concluded it would make a perfect tool for the task at hand. Somehow she managed to drop it on the kitchen floor, shattering the ancient pestle. When my grandfather came home from work and saw the sorry results, he was inconsolable.

The implications of the accident were mind-boggling. Here was an ammonite, which had survived an incomprehensible 190 million years in the ground, as well as a more recent journey through mine-infested waters, only to meet an ignominious end as a failed sauerkraut masher.

Eventually, my grandfather managed to unevenly glue it back together. The beauty was imperfect but the magic remained. I remember seeing the ammonite for the first time when I was around seven. Over the years, I always looked at it with a covetous eye. At the age of fourteen, during an annual family visit, I worked up the gumption to ask my grandfather if I could have it. Without hesitation, he handed it to me with a big smile. The torch had been passed.

Not long after, I made an appointment at the Cleveland Museum of Natural History to show the fossil to the head of paleontology, Dr. David Dunkle. Though I knew it was a fossil, neither my grandfather nor I could determine the species. It was so badly weathered that it resembled a small curled-up reptile. I was hopeful Dr. Dunkle could identify it.

I counted the days until my meeting with him. When the big day arrived, I put on my best clothes and headed downtown. His secretary ushered me into his cluttered office; every surface was covered with fossils. It turned out Dr. Dunkle was one of the world's leading authorities on fossil fish. He even had the honor of having a huge predatory fish named after him—the Dunkleosteus.

I remember his kindly demeanor as I proudly handed him my fossil. He put on his glasses, studied it carefully, and then pronounced his judgment. No, it wasn't some rare reptile. It was something called a *Ceratites nodosus* ammonite. Though I felt let down, I was encouraged by what happened next. Once I told him of my goal to become a paleontologist, he seemed pleased and gave me a pep talk about the long road ahead of me.

We kept in touch. Two years later, Dr. Dunkle said he would recommend me for an annual museum-sponsored expedition. It was a six-week long trip to the Western states, designed for young people interested in the earth sciences. The primary focus was to study the geology of the region with an emphasis on paleontology. With that in mind, our base camp was to be established near Dinosaur National Monument.

Out west, we stopped in Colorado to explore the Morrison formation, well-known for yielding large dinosaurs—Diplodocus and Allosaurus are common. My team of about a dozen students spread out to reconnoiter the land. Before long, I came upon some attractive petrified wood. Then I found a cantaloupe-sized nub of the top of a large dinosaur femur. I was in heaven.

As I started to document my find, I heard one of the kids shouting in the distance. The curator in charge of the trip yelled for everyone to "get over here fast." I trudged up a steep hill and came upon a circle of kids gesturing excitedly. It turned out that Doug Inkley had uncovered a large serrated-edge tooth, which obviously belonged to a meat-eater. This was an important find that clearly trumped my leg bone. I was devastated. In an instant, I had gone from the thrill of victory to the agony of defeat.

That night, as we sat around the campfire, I was tortured as Doug recounted every minute detail of his momentous discovery. My team sat enthralled while I stewed for not having been the one to make the find. I looked up at the stars, wondering if this was a sign from above that maybe I wasn't destined to become a paleontologist.

Now, over thirty years later, the time was drawing closer for me to get out into the field again and hopefully answer that question.

CHAPTER SIX

A Short History of Paleo-Characters

Once my T. rex safari had turned into a solo sojourn, I studied a map and plotted my route from Tucson (where I now lived) directly to Colorado for Mike Triebold's opening. A few days later, I loaded my green Honda Civic, turned onto Highway 10 East, and was off. The roads were empty—it was clear sailing. I couldn't have gone more than twenty miles when my cell phone rang. It was Bob Detrich, the Fossil King himself, calling from Buffalo, South Dakota. *Perfect*, I thought.

"Hey dude, how's it going? You wouldn't believe what I've been finding. I've already got two—count 'em—two rex sites going!"

"Come on, *two rexes?*"

"Richard, I've got to be the luckiest guy on this planet," said Bob in a blissed-out tone. "I don't know which site to excavate first!"

"Well, I'm on the road heading to Triebold's museum opening," I said. "Will I see you there?"

"Gonna try, dude, gonna try! All depends whether the dinosaurs are biting. You make it out to Buffalo be sure and call me. I guarantee if we go collecting, you'll bag a rex!"

"Thanks, I'll be in touch," I said, with no intention of calling him.

As I continued driving, I began reflecting on the history of American dinosaur collecting—a history that went back to Thomas

Jefferson, our first paleontologist. Not surprisingly, even during the infancy of American paleontology, there was plenty of "fear and loathing" among fossil hunters. In one notorious case, a virtual war broke out, the much discussed feud between O.C. Marsh and Edward Drinker Cope.

The two rivals operated during the post-Civil War era when the study of dinosaurs was largely unknown in this country and in desperate need of direction. Thanks to Marsh and Cope it found its compass. When they first met, they identified with one another as kindred spirits and even did a little collecting together. Soon, professional jealousy crept in and they began bad-mouthing each other to the press.

In 1870, their rivalry reached a boiling point over a relatively minor incident. It began when Cope showed some colleagues a skeleton he had found of a Plesiosaur, a large voracious marine reptile. While he was accepting their kudos, Marsh "thoughtfully" pointed out that Cope had incorrectly mounted the skull at the end of the beast's tail. The personal humiliation was so profound that the two never spoke again.

In what many writers have described as the "Great Bone Wars," Marsh and Cope, fueled by family wealth, headed West and launched an unofficial contest to see who could find the most new species of dinosaurs. While all of this was happening, the two men routinely poached each other's dig sites. They were also guilty of something far worse. On occasion, one of them would excavate a location, remove the bones he wanted, and then smash the ones he didn't, thus rendering the site worthless to his competitor.

Despite this ruthless behavior, the rivalry was productive from a scientific viewpoint. Over a twenty-year period, the two fossil hunters were credited with naming 130 new species of dinosaurs, almost half the number of known species at the time. Ultimately, science was the real winner of the "Bone Wars" as Marsh and

Cope's dinosaurs began to fill the East Coast's natural history museums, including the Smithsonian.

Unfortunately, the story's postscript was not as satisfying. It turned out that the 130 new species they discovered may have actually been fewer than originally determined. In their haste to be the first to identify new dinosaurs, a number of their finds turned out to be larger or smaller skeletal versions of the same species. As a result, to this day paleontologists are still unraveling Marsh and Cope's legacy.

While these two characters represent the dark side of paleontology, there was a counterbalance of positive figures. One of those was Barnum Brown, who began his career in 1897 and was named after the illustrious P.T. Barnum. Brown went on to become a showman in his own right, known as much for his longevity—sixty-six years as a paleontologist at the American Museum of Natural History—as for his charisma. A reputed ladies man and accomplished ballroom dancer, he was frequently photographed out in the field wearing a full-length fur coat.

His legacy was the discovery of the first Tyrannosaurus rex in 1902 (he found a second more complete specimen in Montana in 1908). The significance of these events cannot be overstated. The second skeleton eventually went on display at the American Museum of Natural History, anchoring the collection and instantly creating a dinosaur-hungry public. So valuable was this attraction, that at the beginning of World War II it was shipped for protection to the Carnegie Museum in Pittsburgh, out of fear the Germans would bomb major American cities and museums. It was not an unfounded worry. A number of European museums and their collections suffered heavy damage during the war.

In the 1930s, Brown cut a deal with the emerging Sinclair Oil Company, thus becoming the first paleontologist to "cross-over" to the business world. Since oil was a fossil fuel, Sinclair had designed a green Diplodocus (a "long neck" dinosaur) to serve as their corporate logo. To attract customers to their service stations, they hired Brown to write the text for giveaway booklets on dinosaurs. Brown, in turn, used the money to finance his expeditions. He continued to serve as a consultant to Sinclair and helped organize their dinosaur pavilions for the Chicago World's Fair (1933–34) and the New York World's Fair (1964–65), while keeping his other foot firmly in the scientific end of paleontology.

Then there was the legendary Roy Chapman Andrews, considered by many to be the inspiration for Indiana Jones. Andrews may have been even *more* flamboyant than the fictional character. He became an iconic explorer through his manner of dress (pressed safari clothing) and attitude (wearing a side arm and using it to fight off an attack by desert bandits in Mongolia). His personal style and daring exploits made him paleontology's first superstar.

Andrews came to international prominence during the 1920s when the American Museum of Natural History sponsored a series of expeditions to the Gobi desert. His initial foray was a search for fossil evidence of human life—an attempt to find the "missing link." Instead, he found dinosaurs.

In 1923, Andrews returned to the Flaming Cliffs of Mongolia. This expedition, like those past, was a complicated affair. In the days before cell phones, the Internet, and commercial flights, international travel logistics were no joke. Imagine what it was like eighty years ago securing reliable automobiles that would function in a desert sandstorm. Then you had to ship them across the Pacific Ocean. Once you arrived in Mongolia, you still had to hire porters, purchase water, fuel, non-spoiling food, camels, and tents. Another obstacle was an unstable government that offered little protection from local thieves.

In Andrews's case, the real danger turned out to be poisonous snakes. One night, his camp was invaded by dozens of vipers, probably seeking warmth from the freezing desert night. Members of his party woke up to slithering reptiles crawling *inside* their tents. The cook even found one in bed with him. In the confusion, Andrews literally flipped out as he stepped on what he thought was a snake, which turned out to be only a piece of rope. Somehow, in all the chaos, no one was bitten.

The next day, his team spread out looking for signs of prehistoric life. Soon, paleontologist George Olson came rushing back to camp with several oval spheres that he thought were fossil eggs. At first, Andrews was skeptical and wrote them off as a geologic curiosity. Upon further reflection he realized they weren't anything he had seen before. Once he checked out Olson's site and saw other eggs and pieces of shell, he realized they couldn't be anything else.

Although the field of paleontology was already established, no one knew whether dinosaurs laid eggs or gave birth to live young. Once Andrews became the first person to correctly identify dinosaur eggs, he changed the science forever.

While continuing to explore, Andrews discovered a skeleton perched on top of one of the nests. He named it Oviraptor, which meant "egg-stealer." In this case, Andrews *incorrectly* postulated the creature was stealing eggs. Around fifty years later, it was determined the Oviraptor actually laid the eggs. Regardless, the creature's name and Andrews's reputation remained intact.

Word of the dinosaur egg discovery reached New York, and the ensuing press turned Andrews into a hero. In order to raise money for future expeditions, he convinced the museum to auction off one of the Oviraptor eggs. After some spirited bidding, the egg sold for $5,000, an impressive sum in 1923. However, the auction proved to be a shortsighted mistake. The government of Mongolia learned of the sale and immediately determined the Americans were out to steal their valuable patrimony. It took years of negotiations before Andrews and his colleagues were allowed back.

Many years went by until the fossil world saw the emergence of its next vibrant individual, Dr. Robert T. Bakker. Since graduating from Yale in 1966, Bakker has done more to shake up the field of paleontology than any individual in its history. Take his image, for instance. Rather than present himself as a swashbuckling adventurer, he looks more like a member of the band ZZ Top—pony-tail, long-flowing beard, and well-worn cowboy hat. As a former preacher, he developed a reputation as an engaging speaker, who was particularly good with kids. In fact, Bakker became something of a rock star. His "concerts" were always well attended with members of the audience seeking autographs after the performance.

In 1986, Bakker published his radical book, *The Dinosaur Heresies*. Bakker proposed that dinosaurs were warm-blooded creatures, upsetting previous assumptions. He viewed them as reasonably intelligent animals that moved with grace and speed, rather than dull, dim-witted beasts. Further, his book helped advance the theory that birds evolved from dinosaurs. Bakker's philosophy was to treat dinosaurs as unique life forms, neither reptile nor mammal. As he put it, "Let dinosaurs be dinosaurs."

A proficient artist and writer, Bakker penned a well-received novel, *Raptor Red*. The story had a unique perspective. Written from the viewpoint of a dinosaur, it encapsulated a year in the life of a raptor. We follow her adventures in a world filled with peril and hostile natural forces, allowing Bakker to put some of his scientific theories into play. His narrative brought dinosaurs to life, exceeding any *National Geographic* special.

Bakker's real talent may lie in his ability to make the language of paleontology easy to understand. He was quoted as saying, "There's a friend of mine who works on fossil turtles and speaks in sentences like 'the *fossa orbitalas* is displaced in a derived condition rostally.' All it means is the eye socket is near the front of the head. Why not say, 'The eye socket is near the front of the head?'" By bringing this sort of common sense approach to paleontology, along with shaking up the public's perception of dinosaurs, Bakker opened up the science to a wider audience.

Another well-known figure in the dinosaur world, Jack Horner, gained notoriety by serving as a technical adviser for the movie, *Jurassic Park*. More importantly, he distinguished himself by finding the first dinosaur eggs in America, some with fossil embryos inside. His site in north central Montana has yielded so many finds, that it's referred to as Egg Mountain.

Using the Museum of the Rockies in Bozeman, Montana as his base, Horner evolved theories as controversial as Bakker's. For instance, he hypothesized that dinosaurs had strong parenting instincts. Horner's theory revolved around his discovery of a new species, Maiasaura, which means "good mother lizard." By observing its nesting characteristics, such as even spacing between nests, Horner determined the creature was part of a colony that returned yearly to give birth. He also concluded there was a lack of plant life in the vicinity surrounding the nests. This meant that rather than hatch their eggs and leave the babies to fend for themselves, the Maiasaura behaved responsibly, finding food and bringing it back to their young.

Horner's reputation was burnished further when he found a T. rex even larger than Sue, weighing thirteen tons. Along with this behemoth, he found parts from five other T. rexes, indicating they may have been traveling in a pack like giant jackals when they died. From this evidence, Horner postulated that T. rex was more of a scavenger than a hunter. In his book, *The Complete T. Rex*, he claims their nasty teeth were used to bite off chunks of rotting flesh rather than to bring down prey. If this idea gains credence, then our indelible image of T. rex as a ferocious predator may go the way of the dinosaur.

Though Jack Horner and Robert Bakker were the latest in a long series of colorful dinosaur hunters, my sense was they wouldn't be the last. Peter Larson was certain to leave his mark. Then there was the wild card, Bob Detrich. While I harbored serious doubts about his credibility, there was something about the Fossil King that convinced me he might emerge from a cast of boneheaded characters as a figure to reckon with.

CHAPTER SEVEN

Drinking Vintage T. Rex Red

Thinking about all the eccentrics in paleontology helped vanquish the monotony of my drive to Albuquerque. As daylight faded, I pulled into a Super 8 Motel so exhausted that within thirty minutes I fell asleep with the television on. By 7:00 a.m., I was showered and back on the road. Oddly enough, I couldn't wait to start driving. Drawn by the call of T. rex, I motored through the state of New Mexico and didn't stop until Pueblo, Colorado.

By noon the next day, I had made my way to Woodland Park, home of Mike Triebold's new Rocky Mountain Dinosaur Resource Center. Inside, the museum was swirling with activity as employees made last minute preparations for that night's grand opening. I looked up and spotted a technician adjusting the lights on an Oviraptor skeleton so that it cast shadows to make it appear more three-dimensional. Another person was uncrating a specimen in the working laboratory, which was open to public view. And a team in the museum store was making sure the shelves were fully stocked and the cash registers were turned on. The Center had billed itself accurately as a "new species of museum"—it was for profit.

While searching for Triebold, I ran into chief curator Walter Stein who exuded youthful charm along with an infectious smile. He was dressed from head to toe in tan khakis. His shirt displayed the Triebold Paleontology logo depicting a dramatic black Raptor.

Once Stein donned his wide-brimmed hat, he looked every bit the part of the intrepid dinosaur hunter. Taking a long drag on a cigarette, he said, "So, you're really looking for a T. rex? *Seriously?*"

"I know it sounds a little crazy."

"No, no, it's not crazy at all!" said Stein, with great enthusiasm.

"I realize things are a little hectic, but if you can tear yourself away, maybe I could take you to lunch and talk to you about your collecting experiences."

"Sure," said Stein. "I could use a break. Let me just return a call and I'll be ready to go. In the meantime, take a look around."

I was thrilled by the exhibits. Usually, natural history museums catered heavily to children, or they went too far in the other direction. The Center appeared to have gotten it just right, striking a balance between being scientific and user-friendly. For instance, they juxtaposed a mounted dinosaur skeleton with a life-size restoration of what it may have looked like when it was alive. Hung above the two creatures was a wonderful painting by Todd Marshall, offering a speculative view of the dinosaur in his environment.

The Center also found a way to successfully incorporate dinosaurs and popular culture. A room was devoted to reproductions of dinosaur movie posters, including: *The Ghost of Slumber Mountain* (1919), the first film appearance of dinosaurs; *The Lost World* (1925), based on the Sir Arthur Conan Doyle novel; *King Kong* (1933), though Kong wasn't a dinosaur, his homeland was populated with them; *One Million B.C.* (1940), where the dinosaurs were played by real lizards with horns tied on their heads; *One Million Years B.C.* (1966), also known as the "Raquel Welch" movie; *The Valley of Gwangi* (1969), Ray Harryhausen's stop-motion spectacle; and *Jurassic Park* (1993), the Rolls Royce of dinosaur films. The vast majority were illustrated in a primitive comic book style. And they were extremely violent—the malevolent dinosaurs clearly meant business.

Leaving that room, I came upon a cluster of mounted skeletons that formed the central focus of the museum. Triebold and his staff had created an awesome pose of three dinosaurs. A vicious Albertosaurus (related to a T. rex), his jaws straining open as wide as physically possible, was standing in triumph over a fallen Duck-bill, with another Albertosaurus on the way. It was so realistic, you could almost hear the roar of the victorious predators and the desperate cries of the doomed.

I was about to snap a photo when Walter Stein returned. He looked a little upset.

"What's wrong?" I asked.

"We just got word that Robert Bakker canceled speaking at tomorrow's opening for the general public—after all the trouble we went through to book him as our keynote speaker. So now we've got approximately twenty-four hours to find a replacement. How do you replace Bob Bakker?" Shrugging off the setback, he said, "Come on. I know a good Mexican restaurant down the street."

Over tacos and enchiladas, Stein confessed that unlike most people in his field, he lacked an advanced degree. While he did have a B.S. in geology, he hadn't had the money or inclination to pursue a graduate degree in paleontology. Yet, through determination and an intense passion for fossils, he found himself working as a chief curator. This led to the inevitable discussion about institutional collectors versus commercial collectors and who contributed the most to our understanding of dinosaurs. Was it the professionals with their doctorates and scientific theories or the commercial dealers who often had superior credentials when it came to field experience?

For years, the bane of professional paleontologists were collectors who plundered fossils beds by stripping away the specimens without recording any data. The professionals were correct, of course. A dinosaur without any contextual information is virtually worthless. To understand how the creature lived and died, one needs to know what other fossils occurred in close proximity, the identification and dating of the formation, and the placement of the bones as they were discovered.

However, the stereotype of the "careless collector" has become outdated. The bottom line is there's too much money at stake not to do things correctly. Any serious collector knows you can get a higher price for a specimen that is collected responsibly. Yet, most university professors and museum scientists still don't see it that way. They claim there's only so much fossil-bearing land around to allow anything but the most stringent collecting standards.

Their argument has no teeth. There are plenty of fossils around, with more weathering out every day. Common sense dictates that it's better to have as many people out looking for fossils as possible (and risk a few losses), than allowing thousands of fossils to disintegrate because they were on government land and only accessible to professionals with permits. Universities and museums are so under-funded that fossil expeditions are the exception rather than the rule. Our enormous country spends a thimble full of money on paleontology. Ditto for the rest of the world's governments. At any given time there are fewer than fifty paleontologists out in the field worldwide.

Stein explained that the Center's goal was finding a balance between being profitable and educational. He saw his mission as "trying to bring along those in the commercial realm who are not doing it the right way."

"Let's talk about T. rex. When I first met your boss he mentioned that you were excavating the world's first juvenile rex. *

Stein replied, "We are and it's been a lot of work! But we're doing it the right way. By that I mean we found it on land that be-

---

* A year later, in 2005, "Sir William" turned out not to be a juvenile rex, but a dinosaur previously unknown to science.

longed to a university and we immediately drew up a contract—you don't dig on someone else's land with just a handshake. The deal we struck called for us to handle the excavation and mounting, but ultimately the specimen would belong to the university and to us as equal partners."

"So when you go to sell it, you'll split the proceeds?"

"Exactly."

Then he added, almost as an off-hand remark, "What makes you think *you* can find a T. rex?"

Before I could answer, he said, "Are you aware of how few T. rexes have been found in the last 100 years? You can't expect to just go out there and find one! It's not that easy. I essentially got lucky when I found 'Sir William.' I mean, you might find a tooth—maybe a bone or two. Isolated bones are far more common."

I asked, "So does a bone count as a find? How much of the animal do you need to uncover to claim you discovered one?"

Stein said, "That's a tough question. There really is no specific rule or formula. I'd have to say at least five percent. Most rexes that have been found are less than twenty-five percent complete."

We left the restaurant and walked back to the Center. Still determined to line up options other than Larson and Williams, I asked, "Well, do you know of anyone I can hire to take me dinosaur collecting?"

"I suppose you could call the Sacrison twins," said Stein. "They have a knack for finding dinosaurs—in fact, they hold the record for finding the most T. rexes."

"Great," I said. "Let's call them."

Then Stein hesitated, "You know, the more I think about it, I'm not sure it's such a good idea."

"Why not?"

"They're not bad guys, but you might say they walk to their own beat. One of them is a part-time gravedigger. I think the other lives in his car. Like I said, they're different—a lot of the locals refer to them as the 'Bonehead Brothers.' I'm not sure that's the experience you're looking for."

Bonehead brothers. I started laughing, "That's exactly the experience I'm looking for! I can't think of anything better than to be out in the field with a couple of T. rex hunters who are free spirits!"

We had just entered the Center when Mike Triebold appeared. Stein immediately said to him, "Richard's trying to get someone to take him T. rex hunting. I thought about the Sacrisons."

"The *Sacrisons?*" By the sour look on Triebold's face, I could tell he shared Stein's reservations. Now I was *really* intrigued.

Before I could explain, Triebold was distracted by an employee's urgent gesturing.

I finally said to Stein, "Tell you what, if you have the Sacrisons' phone numbers, I'll just call them myself. That way you're not involved."

Stein said, "Can I give them to you tomorrow? I think I have their numbers somewhere. Right now, I've got to get ready for the opening."

"Sure. See you tonight."

A few hours later, I was back at the Center. While I had been to many, many art museum openings, I had never attended a dinosaur museum reception. Not knowing what to expect, I decided to play it safe by putting on a tie and a black Armani jacket. Wrong call. Walking into the party, I saw only one other man wearing a tie and another wearing a bolo. A smattering of blazers, yes, but most men were dressed in sport shirts and their best jeans. The women who accompanied them wore dresses and skirts, but virtually no jewelry, with the notable exception of a platinum blond wearing a cut and polished ammonite necklace. What did I expect? Unlike the art world, which was about pretension, the fossil world was about . . . fossils.

Someone called for quiet so that Triebold could make a speech. With his charming wife JJ by his side, he shouted, "I would like to welcome everyone to the Rocky Mountain Dinosaur Resource Center. I'm also happy to announce that we just sold five Albertosaurus skull casts to the producer of the new *King Kong* movie!"

The loud applause set the tone for the rest of the evening's festivities. A highlight was the wine that was served—*T. rex Red* by Colorado's Carlson Vineyards. The bottle's label featured a "partying" T. rex hoisting a glass of wine. The 2001 vintage was quite drinkable.

I said to the woman who was pouring, "You know, this is pretty symbolic for me—I'm actually on my way to South Dakota to look for a T. rex." She said, "You've got to be kidding. What makes you think you can find a T. rex, *of all dinosaurs?* My husband and I are fossil collectors and from what I understand you need the luck of the Irish to find one!"

I couldn't believe it. Even the bartender was giving me a hard time.

Suddenly, there was Bob Detrich, talking to the dinosaur hunting couple, Fred and Candace Nuss. I strolled over to Bob who warmly embraced me, yelling over the din, "Pretty great, don't you think?"

"Sure is," I said. "Triebold's got a winner on his hands."

"You know it. But I'll tell you, someday I'm going to have a museum of my own. Then you're *really* going to see something."

I clinked my glass with Bob's.

The Rocky Mountain Dinosaur Resource Center had cost around $4 million to construct, much of it borrowed. That translated into a lot of pressure on Triebold to stay afloat. But his ambitions were high, and he was determined to become the number one commercial fossil dealer in America.

Triebold's ace in the hole was that the actual dinosaur skeletons and all of the dinosaur casts were for sale. He'd created what could become a highly lucrative model for the fossil market. He had designed an institution with all of the educational qualities of a museum, but with the tantalizing prospect of being able to buy the museum's contents. There were no price lists, but anyone curious enough could comfortably approach the staff and inquire about cost and availability. The asking prices for many were substantial. For example, a rare Pachycephalosaur (a medium-size multi-horned dinosaur) will set you back $750,000, including a complimentary cast.

It's an open-ended debate whether it's just as satisfying to own a cast (at a fraction of the cost) as the original. It's also subject for speculation whether interest in dinosaurs and the market for their fossils will continue to grow. Dinosaurs "for profit" is a relatively new concept. Regardless, I knew the Rocky Mountain Dinosaur Resource Center was going to be a hit—I could feel it in my bones.

CHAPTER EIGHT

Museum Daze

By eight-thirty the next morning there was already a ticket-buying line snaking around the corner of the Center. Mike Triebold had hired an amateur actor to dress up in a T. rex costume, complete with a long reptilian tail that swayed from side to side, to stalk anyone who came within jaw's reach. Digital cameras clicked away as parents posed their children in the clutches of the fearsome beast.

As Walter Stein and I continued our lunch discussion, I asked him for the Sacrison brothers' phone number. Once again I was rebuffed. He still couldn't put his hands on it. As I began giving serious thought to lowering my sights to searching for a *cast* of a T. rex, my cell phone began ringing. It was Henry Galiano.

"How's it going? I want to hear about last night's opening."

I said, "You missed a good party—less flashy than an art world opening but a lot of fun. If you can believe this, they even served T. rex wine—Detrich seemed to enjoy it. Then, right after cocktails, Mike Triebold gave a speech mentioning how the producers of a new King Kong movie just ordered five dinosaur skulls from him—the audience went wild!"

"Really?" said Henry.

"And are you ready for this? Everything's for sale at the museum."

"That's what I heard," he said. "Dinosaur museums are never going to be the same. Triebold asked me to come out and give him a critique."

"The place is hopping. Big success."

"So tell me, any progress with your search?" asked Henry. "Make any connections at the opening?"

"Not really, although Triebold's staff couldn't have been nicer. They even invited me to visit their junior rex site."

"Junior rex?" pondered Henry. "Well, I guess a rex is a rex."

"Speaking of which . . . there's something I've always wanted to ask you. Has finding a T. rex always been one of your goals?"

Sounding conflicted, he said, "Hmm. I'm not sure how to answer that. Maybe deep down inside I'd like to find one. But it's not like I need to. It's been done. I guess for me it's more important to find a great fossil—the greatest example of its type or a dinosaur that's new to science."

Then Henry started to weaken. "Sure, when I searched around Montana and South Dakota, finding a rex was always in the back of my mind. Especially when I looked around Maurice's ranch. That's the thing with T. rexes—if you're looking in the right area anyone can find one. So much of it's accidental."

After a pause, Henry summed up his feelings and confessed, "Yeah, you might say trying to find a T. rex haunts me."

"If they're so hard to find, why have so many been found since the sale of Sue?"

Henry laughed gently. "After Sue was sold, everyone went out looking. For that kind of money you look real hard! But we both know that Sue's price was an aberration. Let me tell you, right after the sale I must have gotten twenty to thirty calls from ranchers each saying they had a T. rex in their backyard! I talked to every single one of them and none of them had a rex. If someone found some bones, whether they were dinosaurs or something else, they thought they'd hit the jackpot."

"Are these just the ranchers?"

"I also heard from some Indian reservations. It was the same thing—in their mind everything was a T. rex. It could have been a dead cow skeleton—it was all a bunch of wishing."

"Well, glad you called," I said. "Gotta hit the road now. Heading to Hill City by way of Cheyenne."

"Why don't I call Peter Larson and give him a head's up so at least he'll know you and I are friends," offered Henry.

"Much obliged."

Hanging up, I felt fortified by our conversation, savoring the thought of what might lie ahead. Driving through Woodland Park, I glanced at my car's low fuel gauge. That's when I came across my first Sinclair gas station—a good omen. In fact, I had forgotten they were still in business.

Pulling up to the pumps, I was welcomed by a small green fiberglass Diplodocus about twelve feet long. The original dinosaur logo had been designed by famed dinosaur hunter Barnum Brown himself. Several children were riding it and another was doing pull-ups from its elongated neck. It reminded me of my childhood, visiting the Sinclair pavilion at the New York World's Fair in 1964. I still remember putting a quarter into a clear bubble-top machine, which injected a gob of liquid plastic into a heated aluminum mold, producing a souvenir Stegosaurus.

I walked into the station and greeted the young attendant, "Hi, the last time I was in a Sinclair, I was just a kid and I remember how they gave out these free dinosaur stamps. Man, those stamps were great!"

Maybe in his twenties, he looked at me strangely, but said nothing. He was way too young. Undeterred, I asked, "Do you still give anything out?"

"Uh, no. But we do have some Sinclair merchandise for sale," he said, brightening.

"Like what?"

"Here, what do you think of this?" The attendant handed me a toy Corvette Sting Ray. The vehicle's design was from the days of my childhood, the same vintage as the Sinclair stamps. As I examined the green metal car, I marveled at its wonderful details, including tiny Sinclair decals. It also had a rather dashing figure at the wheel—a smiling Diplodocus. "Only $24.99 plus tax."

"Alright, I'll take it," I said, reaching for the car. Right after paying, I felt a little foolish. What was I going to do with a child's plaything?

The wide-open plains of Wyoming transitioned to mountains and pine forests as I crossed into South Dakota. The fresh scenery was welcome. So was the cooler weather. Within twenty miles of my destination, I saw signs for Mount Rushmore National Monument. From there, it was only minutes to Hill City.

Right before arriving, I reflected on my early interest in paleontology and how close I came to making it my life's work. Back in 1971, I was a junior at a progressive high school in Cleveland that allowed students to pursue career interests within the community. Thanks to my budding relationship with Dr. Dunkle at the Cleveland Museum of Natural History, I was hired to work as an intern in the department of paleontology.

I was assigned to work under a preparator about twenty years my senior named Ginny. For some reason, she took an immediate dislike to me. One explanation was that she wrongly viewed me as a spoiled rich kid from the suburbs. Or she may have seen me as an unwanted distraction from her own work. Regardless, there was a clash of personalities.

I distinctly recall my first day at the museum. As Ginny showed me around the lab, she kept giving me these *looks*. Whenever I asked a question, she replied tersely, or gave no answer at all. When it came time to explain how to prepare fossils, she reluctantly demonstrated the use of the air-abrasive unit. A miniature sand blaster, the tool was powered by an air compressor, with an adjustable nozzle that emits a fine stream of grit. By altering the nozzle's width and the hardness of the particles that are shot through it, you can tailor your approach to any type of fossil, gradually exposing the specimen without destroying it.

With a little practice and skill, anyone could learn to remove excess rock and uncover a fossil, but only someone with a sure artistic sensibility can bring the fossil back to life. Having had some art training, I had a knack for doing this, which made Ginny dislike me even more.

Initially, she started me out on plant fossils. If you screwed up a fossil fern, it was no great loss to science. Dr. Dunkle checked on my progress, liked what he saw, and insisted I skip plants and invertebrates. He promoted me directly to vertebrate material. I worked on a Labyrinthodont—a five-foot-long early salamander. The fossil amphibian was a challenge because its skull was unusually intricate. There were an endless number of tiny fissures that needed to be exposed. After a few hours of intense prep work, I was practically seeing double.

One day, the British paleontologist, Dr. A. L. Panchen, then the world's preeminent expert on Labyrinthodonts, visited our lab. Dr. Panchen observed my technique and gave me a few pointers. Then he launched into an impromptu talk on the species, saying things like, "Labyrinthodonts flourished for more than 200 million years and rarely had existential thoughts about the meaning of life. . . ." I was thrilled that he treated me like a fellow paleontologist. Meanwhile, Ginny was privy to the whole scene. Dr. Panchen's interest in me merely increased her displeasure with me.

The final straw for Ginny was the day I showed up wearing a patch on the sleeve of my blue work shirt which read, *Cleveland Museum of Natural History STAFF.* I had no business wearing one since these patches were reserved for the museum's full-time professionals. From the moment I laid eyes on that small piece of blue and red stitched cloth, I lusted after it. Ultimately, I got one by befriending the janitor, Walter Daniels. I remember going up to him one day and slyly asking, "Hey Walter, any chance of getting one of those cool staff patches?"

Without saying a word he walked over to his desk and pulled out a patch. Then he started waving it at me and laughed, "I don't know, Richard, if I give you this I could get into a lot of trouble if my boss found out where it came from."

A few days later, Daniels stopped by the lab and gave me the coveted badge. I held it in my hand, running my finger over the embossed museum logo—a red woolly mammoth with long curved tusks. That night, my mother sewed it on to my work shirt and the next day I wore it to the museum. I couldn't wait to see Ginny's reaction.

"Where did you get that patch?" she screeched. "You have no right to wear that! You're not a member of the *staff*. Tell me right *now* who gave you that!"

I tried to keep a straight face, but just couldn't. It was like one of those classic movie scenes when the drill sergeant tells the inductee to wipe that smile off his face. Only the more he tries not to grin, the more he can't help it.

"Oh, come on. It's not a big deal."

I started to walk away. Before I got far, Ginny yelled, "Come back here when I talk to you! It *is* a big deal! That patch has to be earned. *Who do you think you are?*"

I just kept walking, secure in the knowledge I wouldn't be dismissed because I had the blessing of Dr. Dunkle. Ginny knew it, too. Though we were barely speaking, things settled down and I finished the Labyrinthodont. A few weeks later it was put on display, which brought me great personal satisfaction and reinforced the notion that my life was on the right path.

CHAPTER NINE

Hill City, South Dakota

The main drag of Hill City stretched for only five blocks, so it didn't take me long to locate the Black Hills Institute of Geological Research. A window crammed with dinosaur-related products greeted me, including a stuffed Pterodactyl bobbing from a small bungee cord attached to the ceiling. A former gymnasium, the building had been adapted to house a fossil museum, natural history shop, and work center.

When I asked if Peter Larson was available, the woman behind the counter said, "Peter's downstairs in the lab. Can I give him your name?"

I heard the creaking of wooden stairs as Larson strode up from the basement. He looked a little older than he appeared in photos. Then again, considering all he'd been through, he looked pretty darn good. He was fiftyish, with a full head of wavy hair, a slight overbite, and a thick brown mustache. He wore aviator glasses, jeans and a long-sleeved work shirt. Larson had a welcoming manner, yet there was an edge to him.

After liberally dropping Henry Galiano's name, I told Larson how badly I wanted to find a T. rex. He instantly perked up. "Why don't you tell me exactly what you have in mind."

Carefully choosing my words, I said, "I want to hire you to do a little T. rex 'prospecting.' I know that's asking a lot but I was hoping you might be available—even if it's just for a single day. Of course, I expect to pay you or perhaps make a donation to your museum."

Larson's facial expression was intent, curious. At this point, I was still feeling confident. Henry had put in a good word. Besides, he was aware that I had driven over 1,000 miles in a gamble that he'd be willing to take me collecting.

When Larson finally spoke, he was blunt, "Your timing is bad. It's not that I'm opposed to the idea. But I've just been out in the field for three weeks and have all of this life maintenance stuff to catch up on: I agreed to do some house painting for my folks. I need to spend time with my family. I have a new book coming out—all sorts of commitments."

Despite his list of credible excuses, I could tell he was waver-ing. The temptation to get back into the field was a powerful motivator for a dedicated fossil hunter, and they didn't come more dedicated than Peter Larson.

"The other thing is that it's lambing season. Ranchers hate to have any unnecessary activity going on—it spooks the sheep."

"I understand," I said.

"Tell you what. Since today's Saturday and Monday's Memorial Day, why don't you stop by first thing Tuesday morning, and I'll let you know," he said. "Maybe we'll be able to go."

"That would be great," I replied, suddenly feeling slightly euphoric.

Then I remembered I had brought the Sinclair Corvette with me. Handing it to him, I said, "Here's a little something for the museum."

Larson held up the toy car and smiled at the grinning dinosaur behind the wheel. "Thanks," he said. "I've never come across one of these before."

We walked over to the museum's "Dinosaurs and Popular Culture" display to deposit the car. When I peered inside the glass case, there was an original Sinclair dinosaur stamp album and other treasures from my youth. I especially coveted the oil company's "Genuine Dinosaur Hunting License."

With the Corvette safely ensconced, Larson left me to enjoy his museum. The Institute contained the finest array of T. rex material that I had come across. One of the highlights was the original skeleton of "Stan" (named after Stan Sacrison), the biggest male T. rex ever uncovered. Another was the world's largest Megalodon tooth, which would have made Vito the Megalodon Man green with envy. The former gym's stage also displayed a cluster of giant ammonites (the circumference of garbage can lids) on tall stands that were grouped in a semi-circle, as if they were singing in a choir.

I left the Institute, feeling there was now a decent possibility that I'd go collecting with Peter Larson. Then there was Maurice Williams. But perhaps there were others? I remembered meeting the fossil dealer Diana Hensley in Tucson. Her business, In the Beginning Fossils, was also based in Hill City. Hensley was the first female dinosaur dealer I ever met. Young, thin, and quite feminine with flowing brown hair, she was an anomaly in the macho world of dinosaur hunters.

Finding her number in the town's slim phone book, I placed a call. Yes, she did remember me. But when I brought up the subject of dinosaur hunting, she carefully outlined the difficulties of taking a stranger onto a rancher's land. Still, she agreed to meet me at the Mt. Rushmore Brewing Company. Waiting for her, I ordered a "Politician's Wife"—a local beer with a bitter aftertaste. After a sip, I wondered whether that was the brewer's subtle intention.

When Diana arrived, any hesitancy that she displayed over the phone vanished. She was forthcoming and helpful, filling me in on the going rate for various types of bones. Then she said, "I guess I haven't made it clear to you that I only handle the marketing for In the Beginning Fossils. My boyfriend, Jared Hudson, does the actual fossil hunting and prep work."

I just smiled, handed her my cell phone, and said, "So what are you waiting for?"

Before long, Jared walked in and pulled up a barstool. Like Diana, Jared was about thirty. He was a rugged-looking man, exuding a cowboy's silent strength. He also had the most low-key personality of any fossil hunter I ever met. There was something refreshingly humble about him, and he seemed flattered that anyone was actually interested in his life's work.

After a few Politician's Wives, Jared loosened up and spoke openly of the difficulties of competing with the big fossil dealers and working with persnickety collectors. He reminded me a lot of my own tribulations as a private dealer in the art world.

"Diana told me that you can sell all the T. rex teeth you find for $1,000 an inch," I said. "That sounds like pretty good money to me."

Jared grinned for the first time, "Well, it's not quite that simple. First, the tooth has to be pristine to bring those prices. Second, most of the teeth you find are only the tips, the ones that were shed or broken off. The twelve-inch teeth with roots are only found in jaws, and I've never found one. The biggest tooth I ever found was between four and five inches long."

He continued, "I only uncovered three or four teeth last year. Even though I found other vertebrates, my biggest demand is for rex material by far. But I can also see a day where the public loses its infatuation with Tyrannosaurus rex. Then you'll see the prices for teeth drop."

I nodded appreciatively and asked, "How long do you spend out in the field?"

That question opened the floodgates. Jared was now in his element and grew even more comfortable talking. He spoke about being gone for three to five months at a time. He also talked about how lonely he got, how he carried a gun (mostly for psychological protection), the difficulty of getting ranchers to agree to signed contracts, and how exhausting it was spending an entire day digging.

"So why do you do it?"

He shook his head and grinned at Diana, "I'm sure you've heard this before but I do it for the thrill of discovery. Each day's a treasure hunt."

Then he summed it up neatly, "I love what I do."

Glancing at my watch, I saw it was getting late. "One final question: What are the chances of hiring you to take me out to look for a T. rex?"

Once again, they looked at each other. It was as if some sort of mental telepathy existed between the two of them, which seems common among couples who have grown close from working together.

"Wait a minute," said a beaming Diana. "I have a better idea."

"What?" I said, full of anticipation.

"You should ask Peter Larson to take you collecting!"

Why didn't I think of that?

CHAPTER TEN

The Curse of T. rex

t was Sunday morning in Hill City and time to call Maurice Williams. My cell phone wasn't getting any reception, so I began wandering the town in search of a pay phone, which seemed to have become an endangered species, a vanishing bit of Americana. I finally tracked one down and was surprised to learn that I could still make a call for twenty-five cents. I dropped a quarter into a slot, listening to it set off a bell, as it tumbled into the coin box.

Maurice's wife picked up the phone on the first ring.

"Yes?"

"Hi, Mrs. Williams, it's Richard Polsky again."

"Oh—the guy bugging my husband about dinosaurs."

"Sorry to . . ."

Then I overheard a small struggle for the phone. Someone other than Mrs. Williams had won because the new voice was male.

"Hello," said Maurice, while clearing his throat.

"Hi, Mr. Williams. It's Richard Polsky."

"So?"

Thrown off by his brusque response, I said, "Uh, so how are you?"

"I'm fine. Aren't you the one who's after my dinosaurs?"

Playing along, I said, "Yeah, that's me. Listen, you told me to give you a holler when I was in Hill City—well I'm here and I'm hollering."

"Oh, that's right. I think I did say that. So what do you want to do?"

"If it's all right with you, I'd like to set up a time where I could stop by your ranch," I said.

"I'm kind of busy at the beginning of the week."

Knowing I had to leave Tuesday open in case Peter Larson was available, I suggested, "How about Thursday?"

Maurice coughed, "Hmm. Thursday? Let me think for a second. Yeah, I guess that might work. Why don't we talk Wednesday night and we'll set a time for Thursday."

"Will do—I'll give you a call."

I woke up Tuesday full of anticipation as I walked over to the Black Hills Institute to await Larson's decision. I found him standing in the doorway holding a mug of coffee. He had a harried look on his face and his hands were caked in gray dust. Behind him was a long table stacked with unprepared specimens.

"Sorry—I just don't have time," said Larson.

Just like that, with those six words, my search for a Tyrannosaurus rex had suffered a serious setback. My attempt to hire one of America's greatest dinosaur hunters (and certainly its most controversial) had failed. Despite my disappointment, I certainly understood where Larson was coming from. After all, he *had* been out in the field for three weeks and was entitled to have a life.

Why was the dinosaur world so closed to outsiders? For one reason or another, everyone I spoke to was either unwilling or unable to take me collecting. Everyone except for Bob Detrich.

After Larson turned me down, Maurice Williams became my only realistic alternative. I suddenly dreaded the thought of dealing with him. What did I share with a Native American (and supposedly a hostile one at that) who was almost my father's age and had no real interest in fossils? My negative thoughts started snowballing.

Once Larson had delivered the bad news, he graciously offered a little T. rex hunting advice. As we talked, the conversation inevitably pinballed to Sue. Larson had already written a book about it (*Rex Appeal* with Kristin Donnan), which did a thorough job of explaining his position. Yet, he was still willing to answer all my questions. The most interesting comment he made was that Sue, in reality, was only worth $1 million to $1.5 million at the most. Larson felt that "about eighty percent of her value was due to the fossil's mystique created by the press and me." He also mentioned that Sue had cost him over $200,000 in legal expenses, a debt he was still paying off.

I was surprised that Larson was so open to discussing his experience of being incarcerated. "Although, I wouldn't recommend it to anyone, a lot of good came of the time I was in prison. I finally realized what was truly important in life, friends and family."

Trying to provoke him a little, I asked, "What would you say is your biggest pet peeve with the business?"

He seemed to like that question, "Most people are what I call 'dinosaur dreamers.' They think all you have to do is find a rock outcrop, put a logging chain on a dinosaur tail, yank it out, and sell it for a million dollars."

His answer made me smile, however briefly. When we were finishing up, Larson grew reflective about his addiction to fossil hunting. He described it as a high he couldn't get anywhere else. Sensing he was busy . . . his writing collaborator Kristin Donnan was waiting to see him . . . I decided to wrap things up by saying, "One last question—why Tyrannosaurus rex? What's the allure?"

Larson began glowing.

"Because it's the ultimate!"

His parting words to me were less encouraging, "You shouldn't expect to find a rex—it's almost impossible. I've been doing this for thirty years and I've never found one." Technically this was true. He'd only excavated them.

Leaving the Institute, I stopped for coffee and my cell phone rang. Miracle of miracles, there was reception. It was Henry, and he sounded breathless. "Did you hear the results from the 'Barnum' sale?"

He was referring to the second T. rex to ever come up at auction. Estimated at $400,000–$900,000, Barnum wasn't exactly in the same league as Sue, in terms of completeness and quality. Still, the estimate seemed modest and at least some members of the fossil community were expecting big things.

"No," I said, anxious for details. "What did it bring?"

"Are you ready for this? $93,000!"

"That's it?"

"I'll give you the back story," he said.

In 1997, NOVA produced a one-hour special called the *Curse of T. rex*. Echoing the curse of King Tut, the story outlined the grief that befell everyone (other than Maurice Williams) who had gotten involved with Sue. However, after watching the program, I still wasn't convinced. That is, until Barnum came along.

Unlike Sue, whose epic tale unfolded in less than a decade, the saga of Barnum spanned a century. The dinosaur itself was named in honor of Barnum Brown, who, as mentioned earlier, discovered the very first T. rex back in 1902, near Newcastle, Wyoming. Unfortunately, Brown's "type specimen" (the first of its kind to be described) was only 13.8 percent complete. Once Brown uncovered a more complete specimen (this one had a skull), he gave the first skeleton as a gift to the British Museum of Natural History.

In 1995, a fossil hunter named Japheth Boyce, came upon the remains of a T. rex in the same two-square-mile plot of land where Brown's initial rex was found. He promptly nicknamed his discovery Barnum in honor of his predecessor. Boyce and his partners then spent the next two years excavating their find, eventually uncovering approximately twenty percent of the skeleton. This was not just another T. rex. It was Boyce's unflappable belief that his rex was part of the original skeleton found by Barnum Brown.

Boyce went on the record, "As a statement of scientific fact, it's the same animal." As for proof, he claimed the bones he unearthed were complimentary in terms of their weathered state of preservation, chemical composition, and age. "They have the same geological thumbprints," he said. "Many of the bones found in Barnum appear to match what is missing from the British specimen."

The flip side of the story is less uplifting. For one thing, the bones themselves, unlike those of Sue, were unattractive and not well-preserved. Visually, they're a cipher. They were tar-colored, pitted fossils, unsuitable for display in a good private collection, let alone a museum. But the condition and aesthetics of the bones may have been the least of it.

After finding Barnum, Boyce and his partners sold it to a group of investors for a rumored $500,000, only to have the deal become entangled in a lawsuit surrounding ownership. The only hope for the investors to recoup their money lay in the romantic past. If they could somehow convince paleontologists and collectors that their rex was part of the first rex discovered, then they had something. With that in mind, they promoted their find as a vital link to paleo-history. Unfortunately, the plan to sell Barnum privately was thwarted by the judge, who ordered the dinosaur to be sent to auction.

In retrospect, the sale died the day it was born. It generated little of the hoopla and excitement that surrounded Sue. Instead, Barnum was treated almost like a leper. Members of the fossil trade spoke of it in disparaging terms. Much of the talk centered around how *low* it would go at auction rather than how high. Still, some dealers were convinced it would bring at least the bottom end of the estimate.

Although insiders knew the whole Barnum concept was a tough sell, Bonhams & Butterfields auction house did their best to spin it. The sale's catalog strongly suggested that Barnum was part of the rex in London, without crossing the line and guaranteeing it. The expert in charge, Tom Lindgren (of Green River Fossils), also did his best to sound positive. But he too had to tread lightly when asked to describe the connection between past and present rexes.

Adding to the Curse of T. rex aspect that seemed to hover over the sale, the skeleton was being sold under the cloud of yet more litigation. Barnum was now being claimed as an asset in the divorce of one of the investors. In the auction world, the quickest way to kill a sale is to mention the word "lawsuit." Lack of a clear title is the one thing a buyer will not gamble on, or at least not gamble very much.

On the day of the sale, Boyce was seen strutting around the auction room like a preening peacock. He himself described his manner of dress as "high rodeo drag"—bolo tie, Stetson, cowboy boots, and a beaded vest woven by a Lakota Sioux woman. While Boyce was busy providing fodder for the press, the real action was going on behind the scenes. In a highly unusual move, the court determined that Barnum would be sold without a reserve. Once that became public knowledge, everyone in the audience suddenly became a potential buyer. In theory, you could offer only a dollar and walk away with the prize rex. With that in mind, Henry decided to pursue it.

I asked him about his strategy. He replied, "I knew there was no reserve so I decided to go up to $10,000 and thought I had a legitimate shot at it. If I had gotten it, my plan was to donate the bones to the natural history museum in London."

"You mean you wouldn't have broken it up and sold it piece-meal in your shop?"

Are you kidding?" said a startled Henry. "If I would have

done that, people would have thought I was an asshole! But if I had given it to London, I would have been seen as a hero. The publicity and goodwill would have paid me back 100 times over. I mean, just think about the headlines, "Maxilla & Mandible Owner Flies to London to Reunite Dinosaur Bones."

"Makes sense. But do you really believe that Boyce's rex was part of Brown's?"

"It's entirely possible. It was definitely found in the right formation—it would have been extremely rare to have found another rex in the 'Lance' [formation]," he said.

"So what happened? How did it only bring $93,000?"

"As I said, I thought it would bring much less than that—the bones didn't even look like a dinosaur. Then again, it could easily have brought $250,000. That's what I heard someone was willing to bid who planned to donate it to the University of Wyoming. The university wanted it badly. But the buyer never showed up at the sale, claiming an illness in the family."

"Any idea who bought it?" I asked.

"It's hard to say. Supposedly a group of investors from South Dakota. Why don't you call Tom Lindgren at Bonhams. Maybe he can shed some light on the story."

Later that day, I was able to reach Lindgren, who was stuck in Los Angeles's maddening traffic. I said, "Can you talk? I want to ask you about the Barnum sale."

"Sure, I'm certainly not going anywhere."

I said, "I know you can't disclose the identify of the buyer. But can you tell me a little more about what went wrong. Was it the 'Curse of T. rex?'"

"Whatever it was, I'm not allowed to talk about the sale. The whole thing is locked in a legal dispute. As we speak, the bones are still in our warehouse," he said.

I continued to pepper him with questions, but Lindgren deflected each one, sticking to his story of not being able to comment. Finally, he suggested, "Why don't you try talking to Japheth Boyce."

"That's a good idea," I said. "Do you have his number handy?"

"Oh, wait a minute, I forgot. You probably won't be able to get hold of him. He can't receive calls. Japh only uses pre-paid calling cards," said Lindgren.

"What?" I said. "Then how did you reach him when you worked on the Barnum sale?"

"It wasn't easy," laughed Lindgren. "I had to wait until *he called me.*"

Later that day, I spoke with Henry who was unpacking a new shipment of Protoceratops eggs from China.

I asked, "Do you think there's anything to this 'Curse of T. rex?'"

Henry hemmed and hawed. "There's definitely something to it. But it's more behavioral than supernatural. Sort of like what happened in *The Treasure of the Sierra Madre.*"

"What do you mean?"

"Every time a rex has been found people get stupid," he said. "I call it 'Rex Disease.' There's something psychological that happens whenever you find a T. rex. It just taints everything you touch. You're on a big ego trip and then greed and paranoia take over."

"Geez, maybe it's a good thing you never found one!" I joked.

"I'll tell you, if I had, I'm sure the same stuff would have happened to me. I'm certain I would have acted irrationally." As an afterthought he said, "Did you ever hear of 'Z-rex?' It was so named because it was found on land owned by Mike Zimmerscheid. You see, not that long ago, Alan Detrich, Bob's stepbrother, and Fred Nuss ended up with a rex that was 50-60 percent complete—it was a good one. Everything was fine until they went to sell it. That's when they got a little crazy," said Henry.

"Detrich and Nuss decided that if Sue was worth $8 million then Z-rex was worth $10 million. Only no one else seemed to think so. Their whole approach to selling it never made any sense. Every time someone was seriously interested in making a run at it, they'd raise the price. Or if a buyer left a deposit, they'd renege on the deal."

Henry was just getting warmed up, "They even had Z-rex on eBay, but once again they kept changing the price. It kept going up—from $10 million to $15 million to $20 million. Finally, they boosted it to $30 million!"

"How'd they come up with that?" I asked.

"Are you ready for this? Detrich reasoned that a basic fighter jet costs around $30 million and a T. rex is certainly more rare!" chuckled Henry. "While all of this was happening, Detrich started acting foolish—he got weird. I think all of the press he was getting went to his head. Thanks to his newfound notoriety, Detrich decided to get into politics. He actually ran for senator in Kansas and lost."

At that point, I began laughing. I could envision his campaign slogan: "A trilobite in every pot." I was beginning to see what Henry meant about T. rex psychosis.

"So, did they ever sell Z-rex?"

"Eventually, after decades on the market," said Henry. "But Alan Detrich refused to say who bought it and what they paid for it. I heard that he made enough to move to Hawaii."

I asked Henry for other instances of odd T. rex behavior. "How much time do you have?" he laughed, then launched into another story connected to Barnum. Back when the group of investors had bought Barnum from Boyce and his partners, their attorney contacted Henry to do an appraisal.

As a courtesy, without charging for his time, he told the lawyer that Barnum's remains were only worth about $100,000. According to Henry, upon hearing this, the lawyer flipped out and began threatening him. He told Henry that if he went public with his opinion, he'd go after him. This turned out to be a bad mistake on the lawyer's part.

I had never known Henry to lose his cool. But that day, as he recounted the story, he lost it. Describing the attorney as a slimeball, he told him that just for threatening him, he was going to formalize his appraisal and e-mail it to everyone in the fossil community. Which he did.

It occurred to me that even though Henry never found a T. rex, even by association his behavior had been momentarily affected. Then I wondered what might happen to me if I found a Tyrannosaurus rex.

"Is there a cure for 'Rex Disease?'"

"A cure? There is none!" he cried. "The answer is to avoid the entire dinosaur world."

Then, without missing a beat, he said, "But you're already in too deep."

CHAPTER ELEVEN

The Teepee Circles at Paleo Park

I t was early Wednesday morning and barely light outside. Yet, I was already filled with anxiety because that evening I had to call Maurice. While I rehearsed what to say, my cell phone rang. It was Peter Larson.

"Hi Richard, I had an idea for you. Even though I still can't take you dinosaur-hunting, I know a place about an hour-and-a-half from here, near Newcastle, Wyoming, where you can go. There's a ranch called Paleo Park. They charge a nominal fee for collecting. I think it's twenty bucks. The owner's name is Arlene Zerbst. Tell her that I recommended you. Anyway, I hope that's helpful."

I immediately called Mrs. Zerbst and she was receptive to a visit. I kept thinking how strange it would be to actually find a piece of a T. rex. It was one thing to hire a guide who might know the best places to look for dinosaurs. But to pay a fee to collect on someone's land, in an area designated as containing dinosaur material, didn't feel authentic. It was like going big game hunting in a fenced-in reserve that had been stocked with wild animals.

Once I approached Newcastle, it occurred to me that the rex known as "Barnum" was found there. Another fifteen miles down a roughly graded dirt road, the axles on my sedan were vibrating, and I had visions of a flat tire or worse. *So this is what pickup trucks are for.*

A few miles later I hit the brakes—a small herd of grazing cattle were blocking the road. As a city boy, I had never been that close to a cow before and was shocked by how big they were. These were formidable animals. I honked my horn but they just stared back at me, as if to say, *We were here first—what's your problem?* I decided to wait them out, but ten minutes later, they hadn't budged. Exasperated, I finally pulled my car within six feet of the largest bull. The hulking bovine was almost the size of my Honda Civic. As I began to inch forward, he backed down, and the others followed.

About thirteen miles from Paleo Park, the landscape became more rugged. With five miles to go, the rock formations began to resemble Martian topography; spindles of sandstone topped by circular forms that looked like flying saucers. Near the entrance there was a sign decorated with a line drawing of a Triceratops. At the ranch house, a barking black Labrador retriever announced my arrival, bringing Mrs. Zerbst outside.

She was a tall blond in her mid-sixties, with the drawn look of a lifetime smoker. As if on cue, she lit up a Marlboro. Mrs. Zerbst couldn't have been warmer and offered to give me a quick tour of the ranch. She explained that most of their visitors were families who stayed for a few nights to do a little fossil hunting, ride horses, and hike. At night, meals were cooked in a large communal kitchen and eaten in an adjoining dining room. After dinner, once it grew dark, guests were encouraged to go for walks. I was told the heavens were so crowded with glistening stars that the night sky felt alive. Though dinosaur hunting was the main attraction, the idea was for people to use Paleo Park as a place to kick back and relax.

Mrs. Zerbst introduced me to her daughter, Kristen Stauffer, who was holding a young baby. Like her mom, she was tall with a solid build, strawberry blonde hair, and she'd inherited her outgoing ways.

"I'll be taking you out on the ranch to do some collecting," said Kristen, promptly lateraling the baby to her mother. "We'll go out in the field for about two hours."

"Sure that'll be enough time? I'd be happy to pay extra to stay out all day."

She just shook her head. "Believe me, after two hours of going up and down these hills, you'll be ready to go back."

"Fine," I said. "Let's get going."

Pointing to a large rusting Ford pickup, Kristen said, "All right, let's go have a look."

As we drove down a kidney-jarring, rut-filled road, I said, "Your mom said you grew up here. I can't imagine what it would be like living on a secluded ranch. Didn't you feel isolated?"

With one hand on the wheel, Kristen said, "Not at all, I love it here. This is my home. My grandfather homesteaded the place and it's been in the family ever since. It'll be mine some day and I have no plans of ever leaving."

"Don't get me wrong, your ranch and the land are gorgeous. I just wondered what you did for stimulation. Do you travel a lot?"

"No, not really. Believe me, with two small children I've got enough on my plate. Besides, my husband has to deal with the oil wells on the property. There aren't that many of them but they require constant maintenance," she said.

Changing the subject, I asked, "So have you always been interested in fossils?"

"Always. As a little girl I used to go fossil hunting with my dad. When he was younger, he found a dinosaur that was almost complete. I forgot what type it was. Over the years, when time permitted, he continued to collect. Eventually, he came up with the idea of opening up a portion of the ranch to allow others to enjoy it. That's how Paleo Park got started."

"How about you?" I asked. "Did you ever find a dinosaur here?"

"Technically, no. I never found a whole skeleton. But I did find a four-inch T. rex tooth."

"You're kidding! Can you take me to the spot where you found it?"

"Sure. That's exactly where we're heading."

Suddenly, Paleo Park looked a lot better.

She slammed on the brakes and yelled, "Hop out. Have you ever seen dinosaur tracks before?"

Actually, I had, but only in museums. We walked about fifty feet and came upon a flat piece of sandstone, the size of a suburban driveway, that appeared to have some three-toed impressions. The tracks themselves weren't that distinctive. They were faint and hard to make out. Still, they were genuine. The fact they were left intact, right where they were found, only added to their significance.

"Do you know what type of dinosaur made them?"

"We're not sure. We've had a few paleontologists out from the university and they each have their own theories," she said.

Just then, a tiny horned toad scooted across the track way. I quickly caught the creature and showed it to Kristen. It couldn't have been more than three inches in length and appeared to be a juvenile. Examining his spiked head, I envisioned the horned toad as a miniature dinosaur. I gently placed the lizard in one of the nearly foot-long impressions, enjoying the dichotomy of scale.

Once we were back in the pickup, Kristen pointed out something she referred to as "teepee circles." During her grandfather's day, Indians regularly camped on the land. When they erected teepees, they would haul large flat stones to the campground and use them to secure the perimeters of the structure. I was told these stones were especially useful during high winds. Now, all that were left of the campsites were several circles of stone, each measuring perhaps a dozen feet in diameter.

We got out of the truck to investigate. Kristen said, "When I was a small kid, my cousins and I used to come up here to search for arrowheads. You could still find things then."

"Did you manage to save any?" I asked.

"Sure. I'll show you some when we get back to the house."

I began walking, tracing the perimeter of each teepee circle. That something this ephemeral could survive intact after all of these years gave me the shivers. It was hard to fathom no one had destroyed the site, either unintentionally by taking the stones for building materials or intentionally through vandalism. It obviously helped that the circles were on private land, under the protection of a single family.

We climbed back in the truck and headed for the fossil grounds. Once we arrived at a long series of bluffs, Kristen's truck drifted to a halt.

"This is it," she said. "You're the first person that I've taken out this season so there should be plenty of fresh material that's weathered out."

When I heard that, I felt a rush of energy surge through me. We grabbed our bottles of water and began walking over a grassy field. At its edge, we came upon some gently sloping washes with lots of exposed rock. Following Kristen's lead, I got down on my knees and began searching. It was only ten-thirty in the morning, but the temperature was already over 80 degrees. Despite the heat, conditions couldn't have been better for detecting fossils. At this time of day the angle of the sun was perfect. Almost immediately, Kristin called out, "I found something."

I jogged over to investigate. "See this? It's the tip of a crocodile tooth."

She handed me a pointy dark brown fossil with a smooth semi-shiny surface, that was a mere half-inch in length. To the uninformed eye, it wasn't very impressive. But to me it spoke volumes about the potential of the site. During the next hour, Kristen continued to find croc teeth, one after another. None exceeded three-quarters of an inch. She also found other evidence of past marine life including diamond-shaped black gar fish scales and the occasional piece of turtle shell.

As for me, I wasn't having much luck. My strategy was to skip the croc teeth and other small stuff and concentrate on finding something major. Kristen walked over to see how I was doing. Noticing my plastic bag was empty, she said, "Doesn't look like you've found anything."

"That's because I've been focusing on finding a rex tooth. Where did you say you found yours?"

She smiled. "I didn't. But if you want to know it was right here, exactly where you're looking!"

"Did you have to dig for it, or was it lying on the surface?"

"Come to think of it," said Kristen. "It was almost entirely exposed. No one, not even my father, ever found any T. rex bones before or after. I'm still amazed to this day that I found that tooth."

Who could figure it? While I was aware of the vagaries of finding fossils, experience taught me that where there was one rex tooth, there should be others. Encouraged by those thoughts, I went back to searching. It was now high noon and the sun was starting to climb. Sweat formed under my baseball cap.

Reaching for a drink of water, I continued to comb the surface. Since the banana-shaped tooth of a T. rex was etched in my mind, I felt confident if there was one out there, I'd find it. But after a second hour of looking, I still had nothing to show for my trouble except small pieces of unidentified bone. At this point, Kristen suggested that we finish up and head back. Although I felt the effects of the heat, I couldn't give up. I might never have a better chance to find part of a T. rex.

"How about another hour?" I pleaded.

Kristen shook her head, "Sorry. We really have to get back. My mom has an appointment in town and I need to pick up my daughter from her."

Kristen's voice had an air of finality to it. As I pulled out a handkerchief to wipe my forehead, I said, "Christ, this is so frustrating."

Kristen looked surprised, "Why do you feel frustrated? Did you really expect to find a T. rex tooth? I told you that it was just one of those things. I was incredibly lucky that day."

That's when I realized I was starting to exhibit symptoms of "Rex Disease." One of the early stages of the malady is having unrealistic expectations. Deep down inside, I knew discovering a T. rex was a long shot that could easily take years. And even that would be incredibly fortunate. Now, I was behaving irrationally because I hadn't found one in *two hours*.

Facing defeat, but not quite willing to admit it, I began hiking back to Kristen's truck. She was carrying a small bag filled with her finds. I, on the other hand, was returning empty-handed. I didn't even bother to keep the few fragments of dinosaur bone that I did find. The trip back to the ranch was a lot quieter than the drive out to the fossil site. I managed polite but subdued conversation, but inwardly I was completely disillusioned.

Back at her ranch house, Kristen brought over a glass jar and spilled its contents onto a counter. About twenty arrowheads came tumbling out. Some were damaged, but a few were in excellent condition. I examined one with a purple tinge, marveling at its perfection. It was hard to believe someone painstakingly carved a piece of chert into this delicate form. The fact that it was functional only added to my wonder.

Kristen motioned me over to a cabinet filled with fossils she'd gathered over the years. The majority of the specimens lay on dark wooden shelves. Because of poor lighting, one bone was indistinguishable from the next. The only fossil treated with dignity was the T. rex tooth. It was nestled on a bed of cotton. Kristen opened the cabinet, carefully extracted the tooth, and handed it to me.

As I held it, any thoughts of envy for not finding it melted away.

All that mattered at that moment was the magic of the tooth's existence. Who cared who discovered it? That it emerged after so many millions of years in the ground was cause for celebration. Think of the odds! In many ways, that wonderful tooth represented everything that paleontology was all about. Not only was it a great specimen from a scientific viewpoint, but it possessed the ability to inspire all who held it in their hands.

Returning to Hill City that evening, I gave Maurice Williams a call. This time he answered the phone, saving me the grief of going through his wife again.

"Hi Mr. Williams, it's Richard Polsky."

Silence.

"Do you remember that I spoke with you a few days ago about coming out on Thursday?"

"Right, I remember. Only Thursday's not going to work—I have some fence-mending that's got to get done."

"Well, what works for you?" I asked.

"Let's see . . . how about first thing Friday morning?"

"Sure," I said. "Why don't I get directions from you while I have you on the phone."

"Directions? Just drive to Rapid City and take the highway to Faith. There's not much in Faith, so when you get here call me and I'll tell you how to get to my ranch. And another thing, make sure your pickup has a good spare."

I thought, My *pickup?*

CHAPTER TWELVE

A Town called Faith

The first thing you notice when you enter Faith is not the minuscule size of the town. Somehow, you overlook the single restaurant, though the corner gas station now serves individual microwaved pizzas. Instead, what catches your eye is a crude sign: *Faith–Hometown of Sue and T. rex Capital of the World*. Unfortunately, the sign lies. Sue was not found in Faith, but in neighboring Ziebach County. What's more, she remains the only rex unearthed anywhere within a few hundred miles of Faith, which hardly gives the town the right to call itself the T. rex capital of the *world*.

Yet, Faith is the closest town to Maurice Williams's ranch and where he picks up his mail. Since Faith is more or less in the middle of the state, it does get its fair share of truckers. However, should a wandering tourist stop because of the T. rex sign, he'd be in for a disappointment. There isn't a single exhibit devoted to the famous dinosaur. Not even a tacky life-sized model of the rex. When you get right down to it, there isn't a single reason for that sign to have been erected.

Luckily, Faith does have a small motel. The Prairie Vista Inn offers just the basics: a clean bed, tidy bathroom, and cable television. From my point of view it was an oasis. There was nowhere else within a half-day's drive.

As I pulled my Honda into the motel's pocked asphalt lot, it came to a sputtering halt, clearly taxed from the rigors of the day's long drive. Then I checked into the motel and was greeted by an older couple who ran it. The man was tethered to an oxygen tank, but seemed cheerful, nonetheless.

As I signed the registration card, his wife asked, "So, where you visiting from?"

"I'm from Tucson, Arizona. Although I just moved there from San Francisco."

"Arizona, eh? We've never been there," said the husband. "We actually don't travel much."

Assuming the reason was because of ill health, I still asked, "Don't you enjoy traveling?"

With a shrug of his shoulders, he said, "Why travel? I got what I need right here."

It was one of those comebacks that was an instant conversation killer. I then asked, "By any chance, do you know Maurice Williams?"

They looked at me in surprise. They obviously knew who he was. But by the expressions on their faces, I'd struck a nerve.

"So, you're here to see Maurice?"

"Yes, I am. I'm hoping to do some dinosaur hunting," I said. "I assume that everyone knows everyone else here."

"You got that right!" said the wife. "But Maurice doesn't exactly live in Faith—he lives about twenty miles away."

"That's what I understand," I said. "I was just about to give him a call to get directions to his ranch. By the way, were the townspeople pretty excited when he sold Sue?"

The couple each made faces. Finally, the husband spoke up. "Yeah, I suppose you could say it was a big deal. But it didn't do anything for us or Faith. Maurice and his family pretty much kept to themselves after they made all that money. But that's the way it goes."

I sensed indifference and envy. It was as if the motel managers enjoyed the notoriety of having a rich neighbor but, at the end of the day, the money from the sale of Sue didn't trickle down to the town of Faith. Once again, as Maurice Williams said, "It always comes down to money."

I went up to my room and called Maurice for directions.

He asked, "Where are you so I can tell you how to get out here?"

"I'm at the Prairie Vista Inn."

"Well, what you need to do is go east exactly fourteen and-a-half miles where you'll come to a dirt road—"

"I don't mean to interrupt, but which way is east?"

"You mean to say you don't know your east from your west?" he said, sounding cranky.

I cringed. This was not getting off to a good start. Attempting to turn things around, I said, "What if I continue to head out of town on Highway 212, will I hit it?"

"Yeah, that's right—good guess!"

Feeling momentary relief, I said, "All right, so when I come to the dirt road, then what do I do?"

"You go north about two miles. You'll then see a small road near a one-lane bridge. Don't take it. You want to take the road that cuts across a pasture. But in order to do that, you need to get out of your pickup and open a gate. Then, go another mile . . ."

At that point, he lost me. When I heard the word "pickup," I had already begun to freak out. There was no way I was going to find his ranch with directions like these. I didn't want to interrupt him again, but there was no choice. "Excuse me, Mr. Williams, but your ranch sounds impossible to find. Any chance of meeting me in town and letting me follow you?"

"No, I don't want to do that. I was just in town this morning and don't feel like going back. Tell you what. Just meet me at the entrance of the dirt road. I'll be there in thirty minutes. Think you can handle that?"

Feeling relieved, I said, "That'd be great. But there's one more thing: I don't have a pickup."

There was an uncomfortable silence. Not owning a truck seemed to throw Maurice more than my lacking a sense of direction. "Look, just meet me where I said and then we'll ditch your car somewhere. See you in a bit."

Before I could suggest a counter-proposal, he hung up, and I started to worry. *Ditch my car?* That sounded like a bad idea. So I called the front desk and asked if there was a taxi service. But of course there wasn't. Shaking my head, I began to change clothes, trying to find something appropriate to wear. It wasn't easy. I wanted to strike a balance between looking respectable, yet down to earth. I selected an olive-colored Lacoste alligator shirt and some crisply pressed chinos. Next, I began snaking my prized James Reid belt, with its cast silver buckle, through my pant loops. Finally, I eased my bare feet into pair of Tommy Bahama deck shoes.

With that, I drove off to meet Maurice, passing miles of empty grazing land without a home or a ranch within sight. I was also carefully watching my car's odometer, trying to gauge fourteen-and-a-half miles. Before long, exactly at that very distance—not a tenth of a mile before or after—I spotted a green oversized pickup truck on the side of the road.

Peering through dark sunglasses, Maurice rolled down his window just a crack. I could barely see what he looked like. Then he said, "I see you found it. Follow me." There were none of the usual social amenities. No formal greeting or handshake, let alone a "Nice to meet you."

I got back in my car as Maurice peeled out in a blinding cloud of reddish dust. His monster pickup must have sped down the stone-littered road at 50 miles per hour. It was kicking up so much dust that it was a little tricky following him. A few miles later, he came to a screeching halt. As I pulled up behind him, he stuck his head out the window and yelled, "Why don't you leave your car over there!"

Over there turned out to be a strip of waist-high parched weeds. I gingerly eased my automobile toward the tall troublesome plants and heard the crunch of dried vegetation. My car mowed them down like a wheat thresher. I just hoped the weeds didn't get caught in the car's undercarriage and screw up the engine.

I got out of my car and locked it. As I approached Maurice's truck, I began sneezing, undoubtedly from all of the weeds and dust. The problem was that once I start sneezing, it's hard to stop—almost like having the hiccups. Reaching for a handkerchief, I found myself in the embarrassing position of blowing my nose all over the place. I was making a fool out of myself. Maurice just watched me in slight amazement. About ten sneezes later, he asked sarcastically, "Are you done yet?"

Wiping my nose, one last time, I said, "Sorry about that. Anyway, it's great to finally meet you."

Even though Maurice hadn't bothered to get out of the vehicle's cab, I could tell he was a large man. He had a dark complexion that appeared to have been earned through years of working outdoors, rather than from his Indian heritage. His face was creased with lines that seemed to denote experience more than age. He had a full head of close-cropped black hair, with barely a hint of gray. As he slowly removed his sunglasses, I noticed his brown eyes were blood-shot. Still, he hardly looked all of his 74 years.

At that point, Maurice struggled slightly to get out of the truck. Then he stretched and straightened his frame. I even heard his back crack. Now I got the whole imposing effect—the "full Williams." His crisply pressed long-sleeve shirt was covered with depictions of eagle feathers and other Native American icons. I could tell he intentionally wore that shirt to make a statement. It was if he were saying, *I don't normally dress like this, but if it's an Indian you wanted, that's what you're gonna get.* He also sported a large sterling silver belt buckle, three times the size of mine, that commemorated a recent rodeo.

As Maurice gazed back at me, I had no idea what he was thinking.

"I know Henry told you a little about me," I said, "but why don't I fill you in a bit more on my background. Besides dealing art, I recently wrote a book on the art world." With that, I handed him a copy of *I Bought Andy Warhol*. Maurice took the book and stared at the green self-portrait of Warhol on the cover.

"Warhol, huh? Isn't he the 'fifteen minutes of fame' guy?"

"Yes he is," I said. "Anyway, besides art and writing, my other passion is fossils."

Pausing for effect, I went into my rap. "All my life I've fantasized about going to South Dakota to look for a T. rex. Not buying one but actually digging for one." I was hoping to plant the thought that there was more to my visit than just meeting him. "Along the way I became fascinated by Sue, and like I told you before, wanted to hear your side of the story after constantly hearing Larson's."

The name Peter Larson brought about a quick transformation in Maurice. His mouth frowned in anger. Despite emerging as the clear-cut winner in the Sue custody battle, it was obvious that Maurice still held a serious grudge. Maybe that story about trying to slug Larson was true. While I didn't want to provoke Maurice, if we were to have a frank discussion about what happened, I couldn't avoid the subject of Larson.

The moment of truth was at hand. Whatever happened next would determine whether I was sent packing or we moved forward. At this juncture, looking for a T. rex on his property was the furthest thing from my mind. I just wanted to stay in the game.

Measuring his words with care, Maurice put it on the line, "Before we go any further, I want to know right now whose *side* are you on?"

CHAPTER THIRTEEN

The Dinosaur that Ate New York

was unprepared for Maurice's question. If I took Larson's side, that was the end of my T. rex hunt. If I sided with Maurice, I'd come across as insincere. It was a no-win situation, but I had to be decisive. Meanwhile, Maurice was still waiting for an answer.

"Well, if it were me—if I had been in Larson's shoes—I would have made you my partner," said. "If I'd found Sue on your land and suspected she was valuable, I probably would have suggested that we each own half-shares and split the profits."

Maurice listened intently. Once he could tell that I was through, he pursed his lips. "I agree with you. Splitting it from the beginning would have been the right thing to do."

With those words, whatever suspicions Maurice may have harbored about me vanished. The tension was gone. He asked, "Want to stop by the house for a cup of coffee? You can meet my wife and it'll give us a chance to talk."

"Sure, that sounds like a good idea," I said, visibly pleased.

Then Maurice threw in a little teaser, "Maybe after coffee we'll drive out and look at the Sue site if the river isn't running too high."

Maurice put his truck in gear and within a few minutes we arrived at his home. It was a large ranch-style house, substantial yet modest for a newly anointed millionaire. About the only evidence of the Williams family's newfound wealth was a second souped-up pickup truck out front. There was also a large covered building (half the length of a football field) that he built as an indoor rodeo practice arena for one of his sons. That was it.

We walked in and Maurice bellowed, "Hey Darlene! Come on out from the kitchen."

Darlene Williams was a few years younger than Maurice, with a petite trim figure, glasses that hid her blue eyes, and short auburn hair. She had an easygoing manner, the perfect counterweight to Maurice's tough-guy persona. In person, Darlene was a pleasant contrast with the voice I'd spoken to on the phone.

She said, "Can I get you boys some coffee?"

"That would be terrific, Mrs. Williams."

"Please call me Darlene," she said. "So Maurice tells me you're a friend of Henry's. We really enjoyed the time we spent with him in New York."

"That's what I heard."

"Are you also in the fossil business?" she asked.

"Nope. I'm more of a fossil aficionado. In fact, part of the reason I called your husband was that I'm especially interested in T. rexes. If you have the energy, I'd really like to hear first-hand about your experiences with Sue." Then I added, "You're probably sick of people talking to you about Sue."

Maurice smiled and said, "We are and we hope you're the last!"

"So what really happened the day Sue was found? As an art dealer, if I gave a collector $5,000 for a painting and he cashed the check, we'd have a deal."

Before Maurice could answer, Darlene blurted out, "We were stupid! We didn't know what we had."

Then Maurice piped up. "No one ever believed this, but when Larson approached me and told me he found something important, I immediately told him that it was going to involve the Feds. But he didn't want to hear that and chose to ignore it."

"What do you mean? What did finding a dinosaur on your

property have to do with the federal government?"

"When I bought this property, I immediately put the land in government trust. Since this country has a history of kicking Indians off their land, I didn't want to take any chances. When land is held in trust it means the government takes all responsibility for administering the property. It's kind of like a parent/child relationship. The other advantage is that I don't have to pay property taxes," he explained.

"Didn't that hurt your sense of pride? Isn't that like saying you aren't capable of handling your own affairs? That you need the government to look out for your best interest?"

"Not at all," said Maurice. "It's good business. Anyway, getting back to Larson: I repeatedly told him that even if I accepted the $5,000, I would have to notify the government. I had to run it through them. Like I said before, he didn't want to hear that. I also didn't know it at the time, but Larson had a reputation for gypping Indians out of fossils."

"So you accepted the check. At that point, did Larson think he bought a dinosaur?"

"I don't know *what* he thought. In my mind, I was taking the money to cover the potential damage to my ranch from all the digging and heavy equipment they had to bring in. I sold him the rights to excavate it. I keep telling you this. I couldn't have sold him the dinosaur even if I wanted to without government permission."

"So then what happened?"

Darlene joined the discussion. "When Maurice brought home the check, I was all for spending it. But when my kids heard about it, they immediately said they thought the fossil was worth more than $5,000."

"So, what about the tribal council? How did they get involved?"

"Once the *Rapid City Journal* did a feature on the discovery, everyone knew about it," said Maurice. "The Cheyenne River

Sioux tribal council suspected that the dinosaur was worth a lot of money. What made me so angry was that as a member of the tribe, they're supposed to be looking out for me. But instead, they got it in their heads that the dinosaur belonged to them—to all the Sioux people. But, as they found out, the government was a separate entity from the tribe. They had no right to it and tried to screw me out of it."

I said, "Years later, once the courts had decided in your favor, how did you hook up with Sotheby's?"

"An auctioneer named David Redden, who worked for Sotheby's, contacted me to see if I'd consider putting it up at auction. I told him I was interested, so he agreed to fly out to talk in person. I was impressed with his presentation and the fact he would satisfy all government concerns. He was also willing to deal with the Bureau of Indian Affairs."

"Before you agreed to work with Sotheby's, did anyone offer to buy it?"

"Oh, we had lots of calls," said Darlene.

"The thing is," said Maurice. "The government had appraised the dinosaur at $1 million, so even if someone offered me $999,999 for it, I couldn't take it."

"So do you mean if the bidding on Sue had stalled just below $1 million, it wouldn't have sold?"

"That's right."

At that moment, I glanced at one of the walls and noticed a large framed photo of Sue, taken at the Field Museum. I pointed to it and said, "I like your picture."

"Yeah, that was a gift from the museum. We have all sorts of Sue memorabilia," said Darlene.

"Tell me about your trip to New York to attend the sale."

"Oh, it was exciting!" said Darlene. "We had never been to New York before and were a little overwhelmed. We brought our whole family. All the children came and we had a wonderful time.

I'd love to go back."

"I wouldn't," chimed in Maurice.

"Henry told me that the night before the sale he was invited to a dinner that Sotheby's held in your honor."

"That was special," said Maurice. "There's a private dining room at Sotheby's and they had their chef prepare anything we wanted."

"So what did you have?"

"Well, I told the chef I didn't want anything fancy. I said he could cook whatever he wanted as long as it was 'meat and potatoes.' So I had beef. There was also plenty of champagne."

"Henry told me that during dinner you really got to know each other," I said.

"That's true. Even though I had met him at the South Dakota School of Mines, that was the first time we got to talk. By the end of the meal, we were good friends. I ended up inviting him to come visit us and told him he was welcome to dig at the site. He was the only person I ever said that to."

"So what happened the next day, the morning of the big sale? Were you nervous?"

"No I wasn't," said Maurice. "Our kids were more worked up than I was. Sotheby's picked us up in a limo from the hotel and brought us to the sale. We got all dressed up; I wore a black cowboy hat. They seated us in a luxury box above the auction room. Once the bidding started and we saw it was going to sell, my kids started jumping up and down and going crazy. But I didn't."

"So you remained unemotional? How could you have not been caught up in the moment?" I asked.

"I know you don't believe me, but it wasn't that big of a deal. I'm a rancher. I've been through all sorts of auctions before. Not for this to sound the wrong way, but this wasn't any different from a horse auction."

Then Darlene said, "After the sale, our kids were so excited that they insisted that we switch hotels and stay some place 'classy.' Our eldest wanted to stay at the Waldorf Astoria so that's where we stayed. It was wonderful."

"Did you know that right after the sale, NBC had pictures of Sue on the Jumbotron in Times Square? Can you imagine that?"

"Wow," was all Darlene could say, though I wasn't sure if she knew what I was talking about.

"What did you like best about New York, Maurice?" I asked.

"You know what I liked? The hot dog vendors! One of my kids wanted to try a hot dog with lots of mustard and sauerkraut. Those hot dogs were great. That's probably my favorite memory of the city."

"I'm a big fan of those hot dogs, too." Changing the subject, I asked, "What happened when you flew back to South Dakota? Did the people of Faith give you a hero's welcome?"

At that point, both Maurice's and Darlene's demeanor changed. She said, "Not a thing happened. No one acknowledged it. There wasn't even a mention of it in the local papers."

Sensing their disappointment, I said, "Well, you know how people are. There's always going to be jealousy when someone makes a lot of money."

"That wasn't the worst part," said Maurice. As he spoke, Darlene began to punctuate each one of his points with a nod of her head. "What bothers me is that sign they erected—the one that says 'Faith—T. rex Capital of the World.' First of all, it wasn't found in Faith. My ranch is in another county. Second, after ignoring us, they thought it was okay to use Sue for their own interests. If they had just come to us, we would have been happy to participate and help them develop something. But that's the way it goes."

While I listened, I could tell that Maurice was tired. The T. rex saga was over. It had been seven years since Sue was sold. The money was long since distributed among his two sons and two daughters. Maurice had everything he wanted—a wife, children, grandchildren, a beautiful ranch, and an adventure that went way beyond what most people experience in a lifetime.

Maurice turned to me. "It's still early. What do you want to do?"

Up until this point, I was pleased just to have been welcomed into his home to hear his version of the Sue epic. Here I was, within a few miles of what was potentially the greatest T. rex site in the world. *What an incredible opportunity.* I was perched right on the doorstep of the ultimate fossil collecting adventure.

Then I remembered Henry telling me about the additional rex bones that were found near Sue and my heart started to beat faster. Perhaps there were others still out there. I could tell Maurice was willing to show me where Sue was discovered. I knew if I only had a chance to search the site, I'd find something—something big. But for that to happen, I'd have to put a full court press on Maurice.

CHAPTER FOURTEEN

The Dinosaurs Are Waiting

With little pre-meditated thought, I blurted out, "I know you spoke earlier about checking out the area where Sue was uncovered. I'd love to do that."

"If we can get across the water," interjected Maurice.

"Assuming we can, when we get out to the dig site . . ."

Maurice just stared at me. You could tell he was anticipating what I was about to say.

"I would give *anything* for the chance to search for a T. rex," I said. "You have to realize I grew up in Ohio, where the best you could hope for was finding crinoids [marine animals which resemble sea lilies]. Finding a rex was beyond anything I ever dreamed of. I always wanted to—" Before I could finish my sentence, I cut myself off for fear of sounding like a blithering idiot.

Showing more compassion than I thought he was capable of, Maurice picked up where I left off. "Look, Richard, why don't we first see what the river looks like and take it from there."

"Great," I said, thinking at least he hadn't ruled it out.

As I said good-bye to Darlene, she remarked, "I like that tiny alligator on your shirt. Who makes those shirts?"

"It's a company called Lacoste. But I'll let you in on a little secret—it's not an alligator, it's a crocodile."

Puzzled by my comment, she said, "What's the difference?"

As I started to explain, Maurice walked over and shook his

head, as if to say, *Why are you wasting your time lecturing my wife on your shirt's logo—the dinosaurs are waiting.*

Once we were in Maurice's truck, he said, "Okay, let's see what we can do."

We drove off and quickly found the river. As he had predicted, crossing it was going to be a bit tricky. It wasn't that the water was so high. The bigger issue was the mud surrounding the water's edge. Maurice began driving along the riverbank, probing for a dry spot to cross, but there were none. He came to a complete halt and kept repeating, "I don't know, I don't know . . ."

Then he said, "The last time I was out here, I got stuck and have bad memories of it. I was by myself and it took me almost two hours to get out of the muck. You wouldn't believe what a mess it was!"

I wasn't sure whether to say anything. But I was so anxious to get across the water, that I chose to put in my two cents worth, "I'm sure we can make it if we get a running start. No problem."

Maurice just glared at me. With a sigh and a heave, Maurice looked straight ahead and said, "Let's do it." Switching to four-wheel drive, he backed up his pickup, then surged forward as the tires' deep treads quickly gained traction. With a full head of steam, we hit the water and splashed through. Once we were on the other side, Maurice had a broad grin on his face. "You don't know how lucky you are. Do you know how few people I've allowed out here?"

He was right. I *was* lucky.

"Let me show you around."

We drove over virgin plains lined with cottonwoods. I couldn't get over all of the shades of green: moss green, forest green, olive green, apple green, and other hues. As we covered vast acreage, the landscape began to change. The plains gave way to mounds of raw earth, whose multi-color layers were reminiscent of Badlands

National Park. There were sedimentary bands of goldenrod, terra cotta, and light plum.

"Your spread is gorgeous—just stunning. How many acres do you own?"

Suddenly annoyed, he said, "That's like asking a man how much money he has."

"Sorry, I meant no disrespect. It's just that I've never been on a ranch before and was trying to get a point of reference," I said, attempting to quickly recover.

We drove around in uncomfortable silence for a few minutes. Finally, Maurice broke the ice. "Look up in the sky. Did you see that?"

Sensing his excitement, I stuck my head out the window and saw a magnificent bird of prey hovering overhead. The bird made another pass and got closer.

"Have you ever seen a golden eagle before?" asked Maurice.

"No, never," with some wonder. "This is my first."

"Come on. I'll show you where they nest," he said.

We drove a couple hundred yards to a small canyon. At the rim, Maurice pointed out the raptor's large nest composed of dozens of tree branches. The structure had such great design and symmetry that if it were placed in a high-end crafts gallery, it would have been mistaken for a work of art. Just then, five pronghorn antelope bounded rapidly in the distance. We stood motionless for a short while, observing their every movement. I could tell that even though Maurice had lived here most of his life, he never tired of his land and its inhabitants. I understood why. I was enjoying the panoramic view so much that I almost forgot the reason I was out there.

Back in the pickup I sensed the eagle sighting had lifted Maurice's spirits. So I asked him about his life. He began to open up, talking easily about his childhood. During his late teenage years, like many men of his generation, he enlisted in the military. When he mustered out, he took advantage of the G.I. Bill of Rights to enroll in college and graduated with a degree in something "agriculture related."

Despite his education, Maurice was constantly sarcastic about how little he knew about things. With the exception of ranching, any other topic that I mentioned was usually greeted with, "What do I know, I'm only an Indian."

Then he casually dropped a provocative tidbit, "My grandmother was sixteen during Custer's 'Last Stand' and was in the vicinity of the battle."

Astonished, I said, "Do you mean she was actually part of the greater battle?"

"I don't want to talk about it," he said abruptly. "Let's talk about something else."

Fully expecting to hear an amazing story, I was confused by his quick change of heart. Trying to resurrect the tale, I said, "That sounds incredible. I'd really like to hear about your grandmother's experience. I'm trying to learn as much as I can on this trip about Indian history. I even went to see the Crazy Horse Memorial."

All Maurice could say was, "The Indians have always been stolen from!"

But he still refused to be drawn into any discussion about his ancestors.

My thoughts returned to the present when Maurice said, "We're almost there. Tell me, have you ever looked for dinosaurs before?"

I didn't want to mention my recent visit to Paleo Park, so I said, "I've done a lot of fossil hunting, but relatively little dinosaur collecting. I'm sure you, of all people, can appreciate how hard it is to secure permission from ranchers to let you look around."

"I don't blame those ranchers," said Maurice. "Before Sue there had been other dinosaur bones found on my property. I remember a big leg bone that was uncovered—but it eventually disappeared."

Thinking it might work against me to pursue this story, I said, "Were you always a big dinosaur fan?"

"Not really," said Maurice. "Up until Sue, I can't say it was something that I gave much thought to. Why are you so drawn to them?"

"Many reasons: the search itself, the thrill of discovery, the pleasure of living with something I found."

My answers sounded unoriginal and were probably unconvincing. It was time to make my pitch. "If you were to let me look around when we get out to the site, and I discovered something significant, I'd have the satisfaction of knowing I found it. No matter what happens during the rest of my life, it's an achievement that no one can take away from me. It's kind of like when they interview members of the winning Super Bowl team. The players always say the same thing: *Even if I never win another game in the future, no one can take away my championship ring.*"

"So finding a dinosaur would mean that much to you?"

"Absolutely," I said.

Maurice grinned. "I'll tell you what. Once we get out there, why don't you look around. Take your time. Stay all afternoon if you like. I'll sit in the truck—maybe I'll even read your book."

I just stared at Maurice in disbelief. "You really mean it? You're really going to let me look in the same spot where Sue was dug up?"

"Sure. But remember, if you find anything it's mine."

"Of course," I said.

I was ecstatic. Finally, at long last, I was going to get a clean unobstructed shot at finding a T. rex, at the site where the greatest Tyrannosaurus rex in history was found. It didn't get any better than this. *What would Henry say?*

A few miles later, Maurice yelled, "There it is!"

I looked through the windshield and saw a stretch of at least one hundred fifty feet of rugged hills that might have been thirty feet high. As we drew closer, I saw the blue tarp that marked the spot where Sue was found. My excitement was palpable and growing by the minute. Maurice's offer was so unexpected, that I couldn't wrap my mind around it. This was one of those magical moments in life that I desperately wanted to savor. Maybe this was living proof that I *should* have become a paleontologist.

Maurice pulled up within a few feet of the location. "Here we are—she's all yours."

I got out of the pickup, feeling a bit disoriented. Despite the beauty of the land, I realized that I was in the proverbial middle of nowhere. My cell phone had no signal, sparking a disconcerting thought: If something went wrong, we were a long way from civilization.

"This is rattlesnake country, isn't it?" I asked cautiously.

"Don't worry about it."

I then said, half-seriously, "You're not going to drive off and leave me, are you?"

He chuckled. "Believe me, I thought about it!"

Sounding a bit neurotic, I repeated, "You're *sure* there aren't any rattlesnakes out there, right?"

"They won't bother you if you don't bother them."

Though it was only in the mid-seventies, I could already feel the sun, and I hadn't brought sunblock. I also wasn't dressed properly. Some casual loose-fitting clothing and a pair of hiking boots would have been helpful. About the only thing I did right was wear a baseball cap. Also, from a collecting standpoint, I lacked tools for digging—no rock hammer, chisel, work gloves, or crowbar. But I was so caught up in the excitement, that I couldn't have cared less.

Glancing back at the truck, I saw Maurice open my book and begin to read. The whole thing was beyond surreal. If someone had told me at the start of my trip that I would be looking for a T. rex where the world's most famous dinosaur was found, at a site where no one (besides Henry) had been allowed to search—while the property owner, a millionaire member of the Sioux nation sat in his pickup reading my book on Warhol—I would have seriously questioned his sanity.

CHAPTER FIFTEEN
Pay Dirt

Only thirty feet in the distance loomed the blue tarp that marked the site where Sue was found. When I reached it, I sat for a few minutes, soaking up the vibes. For anyone serious about dinosaurs, this was sacred ground. It was the paleontological equivalent of Mt. Sinai, where Moses received the Ten Commandments.

My thoughts drifted to what happened to Sue during her last day on Earth. I envisioned a regal but aging beast (*Rex Appeal* estimated her age at 100), the height of the two-story house I grew up in, patrolling Maurice's ranch in search of prey. But sometimes the hunter becomes the hunted. We know Sue survived a previous violent encounter, thanks to skeletal evidence, which indicated wounds that healed. On the day she died, there was a strong possibility that she was attacked by an individual or pack of rival meat-eaters. It's conceivable that a member of her own species did her in. But whatever it was that got her, Sue probably expired on the very spot on which I now sat.

Trying to fully grasp the moment, I ran my hand across the gray mudstone, breaking off bits and rubbing them between my fingers until they crumbled. I needed something tangible to convince me this was all real.

Henry Galiano had told me that when he came out here, within an hour of searching, he discovered a dinosaur skeleton that he believed was completely new to science. Over the course of three more visits, he fully excavated the beast. It now resided in Maurice's barn where it awaited the opportunity to be mounted and exhibited. But despite Henry's intuition that there were other rexes in the vicinity, he hadn't found one.

Now it was my turn.

I felt overwhelmed and didn't know where to search first. Usually, your best strategy is to look along the ground for anything that's weathered out. I decided to follow Susan Hendrickson's approach of looking upward for anything protruding from the cliffs. My eyes scanned the sheer walls of variegated baked clay. Up and down, up and down. I walked fifty feet, another fifty, and then a final fifty. Nothing.

Despite Maurice's generous offer "to take my time," I felt tremendous pressure to work quickly. Realistically, I probably had about two hours. Paleontology is about patience. A dinosaur expedition usually lasts a minimum of *two weeks* and can often span an entire summer. The first day alone is usually spent just trying to get an overview of the site. You don't even consider digging. Instead, you explore the surface hoping to locate traces of bone.

If I came upon an isolated T. rex tooth lying on the ground, I wasn't about to conduct a full-blown excavation. I was simply going to reach down and snatch it up. The odds against that happening were steep. On the other hand, anything can happen once you're in the field. Just one little distraction, such as a fly landing on your face, can force you to turn your head and completely miss a bone, or lead you to the find of a lifetime.

I periodically glanced back at Maurice to make sure he was occupied. If ever there was a time to be selfish, this was it. Initially, I tried to focus on the immediate area where Sue was found. After only thirty minutes, within a few yards of that spot, I came across a trickle of dinosaur bones that appeared to have cascaded down a small gully. Each tan fragment was perhaps two-inches long, with a smooth surface and the fine texture of bone. I looked for a honeycombed center, which would have indicated it was a T. rex. But these bones were solid. They could have been from a Triceratops, which were plentiful in the area, or some species I had never heard of.

I dropped to my knees and began crawling. It was now one o'clock and the angle of the sun made it hard to differentiate the multitude of scattered rocks from the fossils. It was so tough to see that I removed my sunglasses. Although less comfortable, it made it easier to detect fossils by revealing their true colors and forms. I started to locate more fragments of bone, hoping they might have bled from the main skeleton.

I climbed one of the hills, carefully placing each foot into whatever natural crevice I could find. With each step, displaced stones and crushed dirt slid down the hillside. After climbing about ten feet, I came across the tip of a narrow tooth. For a split second, I thought I had done it. But a closer inspection revealed a piece that measured only half-an-inch in length, far too small to have been part of T. rex's cutlery. It may have been a crocodile tooth and seemed significant enough to show Maurice. Besides, I was getting dizzy and needed a break. I had neglected to bring drinking water.

Finding Maurice with his head in my book, I said, "Hey, look what I found!"

Grasping the tooth between my thumb and forefinger, I carefully handed it to him. Maurice took off his reading glasses to examine the fossil. "What do you think it is?" he asked.

I don't know for sure, but if I had to guess, it's crocodile."

"What do you want to do with it?"

"Why don't we send it to Henry. He could probably identify it," I said.

"Good idea," said Maurice, slipping it into his top pocket.

Then he said, "Did you find anything else?"

"Not much—a bunch of small bone fragments. But nothing of any real quality."

"Well, don't give up!" he said.

I couldn't resist asking, "How's the book coming?"

Maurice shrugged, letting his body language do the talking.

With that, I headed back for round two. Trying to ignore my growing thirst, as well as my clinging sweat-soaked shirt, I searched a different area and quickly came upon petrified wood fragments—a good sign. Dinosaur bones were frequently found in the same geological layer as fossil wood. I kept telling myself that there was a rex just waiting to be released from its multi-million-year-old tomb.

After picking up more pieces of petrified wood, I eventually covered the entire lower ridge of the site, all fifty yards. If there was a theropod hidden somewhere, it probably lay buried in the tons of rock-hard clay and sandstone that made up the formation. At the very least I would need a Bobcat or another earth-moving machine to get down to it.

I had now passed the two-hour mark and was running on pure adrenalin. So far my Warhol book was keeping Maurice occupied. For lack of a better plan, I circled back to the blue tarp. I was haunted by Peter Larson's comment about how after searching for approximately thirty years he had never found a rex. Who was I to think that I could casually uncover one in a single afternoon?

So, of course, what happened next? Looking to my left, I noticed two fist-sized chunks of weathered purplish-black bone. They were each perched on a "tray" of hardened brown clay as if they were being formally served to me. I gently pried one off its pedestal and instantly saw that the center was riddled with hollow capillaries. Could it be?

I pumped my fist in victory. But just to be on the safe side, I removed the second fragment. It, too, had the internal anatomy I was hoping for. Then again, I wasn't certain what actual "camellate" structure looked like. I began telling myself I had found part of a T. rex. Given their appearance and proximity to Sue's grave, it was entirely possible.

At that point, I couldn't search further without tools. There was nothing left to do but remove the two fossilized bones and show them to Maurice. I was reluctant to tell him that I'd found another T. rex. Obviously, I didn't know for certain. But I wanted to believe it. I had become what Peter Larson had railed against, a "dinosaur dreamer."

I was all smiles as I approached the green pickup. When I was within ten feet, I yelled, "Hey, Maurice. I found a few more bones."

Carefully handing him the heavy pieces, I watched him hold each one up to the light, as if he were trying to determine their value.

"Any idea what they are?" he asked.

Rather than say something premature, I simply said, "It's hard to say."

Maurice grinned. "Maybe we've got another T. rex! Boy, wouldn't that be something? Do you think it's possible?"

"I have a feeling that when it comes to your ranch, anything's possible. You've got to be one of the luckiest people I know."

"Maybe so," said Maurice. "What do you want to do now?"

Glancing at my watch, I saw it was almost close to four o'clock. Since I was on Maurice's schedule, I figured it was better to let him determine the agenda.

"I'm up for anything you want to do. You've been more than generous with your time," I said.

Looking me straight in the eye, he remarked, "I have an idea. Why don't you buy my wife and me dinner?"

"I'd be delighted to," I said, happy for the opportunity to reciprocate.

The drive back to his ranch went by quickly. My head was spinning with thoughts of what I had found. I began thinking that maybe it was a mistake to show Henry the two bone fragments. The way I figured, if he never saw the fossils, then he couldn't dispute my T. rex claim.

I said to Maurice, "You know, on second thought, maybe we should just send Henry the tooth. Those two other bones are so weathered that they're probably not worth the postage to ship them."

He thought for a moment and said, "Nah, go ahead and send them. Don't you want to know what they are? You don't want to be a counterfeit." This was a term Maurice used to describe people who were phonies.

He was right. I would leave it up to fate to determine whether I found part of a T. rex—fate and Henry.

Maurice's truck came to halt at a fence with a long gate. "Do me a favor. Hop out and unlatch the gate."

I got out of the pickup and walked over to the rusted wire barrier. With great difficulty, I tried to slip the tangled knot off the post, but failed to budge it.

Maurice yelled, "No, no, that's not how you do it! Where did you grow up? All you have to do is lift the post up. Treat it like a peg."

For some reason, I was having trouble understanding his instructions. I panicked a bit, not wanting to embarrass myself by failing to open a simple gate. This wasn't rocket science. I could tell Maurice was growing aggravated.

"Do I have to get out of this truck?" screamed Maurice.

"No—I'll get it in a minute," I yelled back.

Summoning all of my strength, I grasped the wooden post at the bottom and yanked straight upward. Miraculously, it did what it was supposed to do. Flush with triumph, I swung the post around and opened the gate.

"About time," said Maurice.

We headed straight for the river and crossed it with ease. On the other side, Maurice said, "Do you remember where we left your car?" Hoping he was kidding, I just stared at him. When we found it, I was relieved to see it in one piece and gave Maurice a thumbs up.

Darlene greeted us with an offer of a cold drink. Feeling much better after draining a tumbler of iced tea, I asked if I could go outside to wash off my finds. Besides the two "T. rex" fossils, I had also brought back around twenty small pieces of dinosaur bone to distribute as souvenirs to my friends. As I turned on the garden hose, I barely wet the pair of "T. rex" fragments. If I was right about them, then they needed to be professionally cleaned. As for the croc tooth, I didn't bother cleaning it for fear of losing it. To that end, I asked Darlene for a Ziploc bag for safekeeping.

After rinsing and packing the fossils, I walked back into the house to find Maurice had already changed clothes, now sporting yet another garment with a colorful Indian motif.

"Nice shirt," I said. "Would you mind if I shot a few pictures of you and Darlene just as a remembrance?"

Maurice said, "Fine with me. Tell you what, would you like me to put on a war bonnet?"

Not knowing whether he was serious, I said, "No, that won't be necessary."

"I have one, you know," he said.

Maurice's head ringed in eagle feathers would have made a hell of a photo, but I didn't want to risk insulting him. Somehow, I suspected he didn't think the Indian stereotype was as funny as he let on. Once we were in front of the house, I snapped a few pictures *sans* headdress. Then, we were off to Faith's lone restaurant, a steak house with the whimsical name Chances Are.

As we walked in, a young woman immediately recognized Maurice. She was the daughter of Ruth Mason, who owned the neighboring fossil-bearing ranch. It had been dubbed the Ruth

Mason Bone Quarry by Peter Larson. The spread earned its moniker from its vast deposit of Duckbill fossils, said to number in the thousands. Larson and Susan Hendrickson had learned of the dinosaur yielding potential of Maurice's ranch through the Masons.

Ruth's daughter hugged Maurice and joked. "Aren't you the guy who found a few bones on his property?"

I could tell that her allusion to his big score made him uncomfortable. Maurice forced a smile and we sat down to dinner. Unlike most steakhouses, Chances Are didn't strive to create a Western atmosphere. It was the real deal. We all ordered the same thing: T-bone steaks, baked potatoes with plenty of sour cream and chives, Texas toast, and iceberg lettuce salads with ranch dressing. Maurice and I also ordered beers, specifying "long-necks."

After slaking his thirst with a long swig, Maurice let out a violent belch. Startled, I looked around to neighboring tables, expecting a reaction. Only there wasn't one. Slicing off large pieces of steak, Maurice made fast work of his meal. There was little conversation. I asked Darlene how the two of them met. She responded, "At a dance."

"Were you introduced?" I asked.

"We were, but I told him I didn't want to dance with him," she reminisced, while Maurice listened impassively.

Laughing, I said, "Why didn't you want to dance with him?"

With little emotion, Darlene said, "Why should I?" Then she added, "Maurice had come with a friend and he told me that Maurice was a good guy and that I should dance with him. So I eventually did."

Meanwhile, Maurice ate his meal in silence. Trying to liven up the conversation, I said to Darlene, "So did the windfall from Sue change your lives?"

"Not really. What's nice, though, is that when our grandchildren call and ask for money for school and such, we can help them out."

With that comment, Maurice perked up, "They're always calling."

We had come to the end of our dinner. As we said our good-byes, Maurice's parting words to me were, "Let me know what Henry says about those fossils."

CHAPTER SIXTEEN

So Much for Immortality

The next day, I began the long drive home to Tucson. In Rapid City, I found a FedEx drop-off box and shipped the tooth and the two possible T. rex fragments to Henry. I also enclosed a short hand-written note that was concise and to the point. It read: "Is it or isn't it?"

I placed the outcome of my T. rex expedition in Henry's hands because, as Maurice had said, I didn't want to be a counterfeit. Still confident, I was even formulating plans for a follow-up visit to look for the rest of the creature on Maurice's property. Since it was tradition to name the rex after the person who discovered it, I envisioned seeing the name "Richard" in future dinosaur books. Then there were the requisite lectures and interviews, perhaps a visit from the Discovery Channel and an appearance on *Larry King*.

Late the next afternoon, my cell phone began to ring. I recognized the phone number on its digital display. With a surge of adrenalin, I answered, "Hi, Henry. Well?"

"No T. rex."

"Say that again."

"Sorry, Richard—no T. rex."

In a mounting state of disbelief, I pleaded, "Are you sure?"

"Of course I'm sure."

There was a long moment of silence.

"Well, what did those bones I sent you turn out to be?"

Henry responded, "They were so weathered that it's hard to say. Knowing the locality, if I had to venture a guess I'd say they're from a Triceratops. But if it will make you feel any better, the tooth *was* from a crocodile."

"At least I got that one right," I said. "What really bugs me was that I was so certain I had found part of a rex. Remember, when you told me there were traces of other rexes at the Sue site? Are you *sure* those two bones I found couldn't have been part of that evidence? You just said they were so weathered you couldn't make a positive identification."

"True—but they're still not from a rex. There may be other rex bones out there, but you didn't find them," said Henry, in a tone indicating the discussion was over.

"There goes my chance of having a Tyrannosaurus rex named after me . . ."

"Tell you what," said Henry. "I have a nice T. rex tooth for sale and it's only $1,600. If you buy it, I promise to name it after you!"

Growing despondent, I ignored his wisecrack. "Now what am I going to do?"

"Come on, cheer up. Why not focus on all the cool experiences you had?" suggested Henry.

I did focus on them, which was why I couldn't give up the quest. The challenge was more tantalizing than ever. My first inclination was to call Maurice and ask for another shot. Maybe with a little tact, and a few more steak dinners at Chances Are, I could convince him to let me search his ranch for two weeks rather than two hours. I sensed Maurice was hungry for another score—not so much for the money but for the action.

Then again, Maurice had already extended himself. A day showing me around his property was one thing, allowing me to stay for a few weeks was another. The logistics of spending fourteen days in the field were complicated. I could commute from Faith—that was no problem. Then I would need to rent a pickup to get out to the site. There was also the matter of securing a Bobcat for excavation purposes—which might take *two weeks* to learn how to operate. Besides, Maurice once made it clear to Peter Larson that he didn't want his property torn up. He only let him dig out Sue once it was determined she was valuable.

Asking Maurice for a second chance just didn't feel right. There was also a deeper issue. I still had not resolved the personal "destiny" question. I wanted to determine whether I belonged in paleontology. Now that my T. rex search had ground to a halt, there was a disturbing sense of not knowing.

I knew if I had become a paleontologist, I would have gone the commercial collector route, a direction oriented toward being out in the field. But I realized I hadn't spent enough time scouring the badlands. Embarrassingly, I had only spent a few hours at Paleo Park and a few more at Maurice's ranch. I needed to "dig deeper." I had to return to the dinosaur hunting grounds. Which meant I was back at square one. I still lacked a guide.

While Henry was my first choice, his availability was limited due to the rigors of running a shop in New York. The top commercial collectors, like Triebold and Larson, were also far too busy. Despite their kindness, they protected their turf, and rightfully so. As Henry had explained earlier, "you're not one of us." Unless I could find a commercial collector who would trust me from the word go, I was out of luck. But where would I find such an individual?

Maybe this really was the end of the road.

PART TWO

THE FOSSIL KING RETURNS

CHAPTER SEVENTEEN

Roaming in Buffalo, South Dakota

You're riding with the King!" yelled Bob Detrich. *"How does it feel?"*

Well, it felt pretty good—good and bumpy, that is. I was bouncing around in a pickup truck, scouring the badlands of South Dakota with possibly the only person in America who hunted dinosaurs full-time for a living. Though there are many professional paleontologists, and perhaps fifty commercial fossil dealers, Bob's love of dinosaurs had taken a different path. He had yoked his life and financial survival to the vagaries of being out in the field, beginning each morning with the bone hunter's mantra, "Today's the day I bag a T. rex!"

As Bob's white pickup hit a deep rut in a long-dry dirt road, he shouted, "I'm a fossil terrorist! I'm a fucking fossil terrorist!"

After months of wondering what went wrong with my expedition, I finally came to grips with reality. I'd been unable to penetrate the inner circle of dinosaur hunters. I was prepared to go back on the road for however long it took, but I needed the right bone hunter. It had to be someone aggressive—someone not deterred by the steep odds—someone fanatical enough to believe that each time he was out in the field he would unearth a fantastic dinosaur. That's when I decided to call the Fossil King.

Before contacting Bob Detrich, I phoned Henry Galiano,

looking for approval. I said, "Do you think I should just get it over with and call Detrich?"

With a slight chuckle, he responded, "Definitely. Bob finds a T. rex *every week*—sometimes two!"

I had to laugh. "I sense the fossil market is in a lull right now. From what I can see there's no juice—no action. What do you think's going on?"

Skipping a beat, Henry spoke, "Well, the fossil market, like most collectibles markets, is event driven. You had *Jurassic Park*, which was a huge catalyst for business. Then you had Sue. Sort of a one-two punch. But now there's really nothing driving the field."

Henry's comments rang true. Without a major happening, there was little to encourage new collectors to enter the market. Sure, there would always be people building fossil collections, much like coin and stamp collectors. After *Jurassic Park*, there were new individuals inspired to buy a dinosaur femur for their home. Once the movie faded from the consciousness of popular culture, so did the market for dinosaur femurs. Ditto for rex material after the slew of publicity surrounding Sue died down.

By 2005, there was nothing to stoke the industry. What was needed was a blasting cap. Something analogous to the discovery of a living fossil, such as the hoopla over a live Coelacanth—a prehistoric fish considered to have died off millions of years ago—which was found swimming off the Comoro Islands in 1937.

I asked Henry, "What would happen if someone found a T. rex *egg*?"

"That might do the trick," he mused.

Nobody had ever found a T. rex egg, or better yet, one with a fossilized embryo inside. The financial implications were tremendous. A bona fide T. rex egg with an embryo might bring a price that would put Sue to shame.

Swallowing hard, I finally called Bob Detrich in Buffalo, South Dakota. I caught him in the middle of operating his trusty Bobcat. Over the purring of the machine's engine, he yelled, "Hey, I was expecting your call!"

"You were?"

"Sure. I knew you'd eventually come to your senses and call me!"

"You were right, Bob," I sighed. "I want to hire you to help me get a T. rex. Can we work something out?"

"Of course we can. What you need to do is get your ass up here as soon as possible. I've already got two rex sites going, so if you want to be part of history . . ."

"I could probably be there next week. Would that be too late?" I asked.

"No, no, not at all. By then the Sacrisons should be back in town. You know they're part of my team."

The Sacrisons—at long last. "I've been dying to meet those guys. I understand they've got some sort of sixth sense when it comes to finding T. rexes."

There was silence.

"Bob, are you there?"

"Yeah, I'm here. Just remember *I'm* the King—not the Sacrisons. You got it?"

"Sorry. What I meant to say was it would be fun to meet them, but you're the one calling the shots."

"All right, then!"

With that, I signed off.

Though I was elated, I also wondered what I was getting myself into. Henry had said Bob was a hard worker who found a fair number of fossils, yet his colleagues had a difficult time taking him seriously—and so did I. That's when I decided to test him.

At the Field Museum's gift shop I'd once seen an excellent cast of one of Sue's twelve-inch teeth. Virtually every crack and imperfection was faithfully reproduced, from the serrated edges to its dense brown color and enamel-like surface. I called the gift shop and bought it.

Once I was in the badlands, I would sneak the faux tooth from my jacket and bury it, leaving the tip barely exposed. There was no doubt in my mind Bob would fall for the gag. I could just see the look on his face. Better yet, I might offer to buy it from him while it was still in the ground. This was going to be good.

Arriving in Buffalo (population 380), I checked into the Tipperary Lodge Motel. Rather than being named for the Irish town, the name honored a famous local horse. The lodging was also a bargain, with rooms going for $38.05 a night.

A few minutes later Bob met me in the lobby and vigorously pumped my hand. "You made it!"

Over six feet, Bob was in his early forties but looked younger. A good-looking man, he'd once sheepishly disclosed to me that he had been a fashion model. He smiled easily, projecting a boyish charm.

"You made it!" he said again.

"Yeah, it's been a long schlep, but it's good to be here. Where are the dinosaurs?"

"Oh, they're out there! Are you ready for this? I think I've got *another* rex site!"

Before I could respond he handed me a paper bag.

"What's this?"

Grinning, Bob said, "I've got a little something for you—something to welcome you to this part of the country."

Reaching into the bag, I pulled out a survival knife, still in its protective sheath. It had a bright orange sure-grip handle and a formidable blade.

Gently touching its edge, I remarked, "That's quite a knife—I feel like I fit in already." I immediately attached it to my belt.

"Absolutely," said Bob, visibly pleased by my response. "What do you say we head over to the No. 3?"

"What's that?"

"You'll see."

We walked outside, under a cold moonlit sky. A spooky penumbra surrounded the glowing disc. We hopped into Bob's white pickup and made the short drive to the No. 3, Buffalo's only bar. Once I pushed open the screen door, all of the activity came to a halt. It took me a few seconds to I realize everyone was looking at me. There must have been at least a dozen cowboys seated at the bar, plus a handful of others around the tables. Above the bar was a stuffed mountain lion, posed ready to pounce.

That's all I had time to take in, as I said, "What's wrong? What'd I do?"

One of the men barked, "You're inappropriately dressed!"

Looking myself over from top to bottom, I said, "What do you mean? I'm wearing boots, jeans . . . What the hell's wrong with—"

Then the cowboy tapped the top of his head.

Still mystified, I said, "Yeah, I'm bald. So what?"

"Your head's uncovered. Better put on a cap!"

With that the bar came back to life with assorted smirks, grunts, and laughter.

Bob said, "Come on, they sell caps here—why don't you buy one?"

I motioned to the woman tending bar. She leaned over the bar, pressing her breasts against the wooden railing. She was wearing a blouse with two or three buttons undone that revealed ample cleavage. I must have stared a beat too long because she said, "My eyes are up here."

Feeling foolish for falling into her trap, I said, "Sorry about that. Let me have one of those No. 3 caps—the black one with the red stitching."

She pulled a cap off a rack on the wall. Once I adjusted its back strap and covered my head, I felt a lot better. "What do you have on draft?"

"No draft—only bottles. Do you want a Coors or a Bud?"

I thought, *What, no micro-brews?* Then I turned to Bob, "What'll it be?"

"Bud." Then he turned to the bartender, "Sandy, keep a tab open, would you honey?"

"Sure, handsome."

The next thing I knew, Bob began circulating, glad-handing left and right. Even though he was based in Kansas, he was treated as a local and seemed well-liked. I learned later that he had gone out of his way to ingratiate himself. Every year, Bob funded four $500 scholarships for Buffalo school children. He also patronized the town's businesses, careful to blend in rather than stand out. Bob had excellent manners and treated everyone with respect. In Buffalo that took you a long way.

Three Buds later, a young—make that very young—woman wandered over to Bob and began flirting. Though she wore a wedding band, she clearly had a thing for him. Bob whispered, "Are you sure you want to be doing this?"

She replied, "I'm in trouble with my husband anyway!"

"Hey Richard, I want you to meet Turkey Ridge."

Turning to her, I said, "Come on—that's not your real name."

"Sure is—and my father's name is Eagle Ridge."

"Eagle Ridge?"

"Where you from, anyway?" she asked.

"I'm from San Francisco."

I must have said it fairly loudly, or at least loud enough to hear over the jukebox—incongruously playing the Blue Oyster Cult's, "Don't Fear the Reaper." That's when someone with an imposing glare looked over at me. Nudging Bob, I asked who he was.

"That's John Carter."

"What's he do?"

"He's a carpenter," said Bob. "But he's also a bone hunter and pretty good at it."

Carter pulled up a chair. Slurring his words, he pointed at me and asked, "Are you buying?"

"Sure, I'll buy you a beer," I responded. With that our waitress brought over three more Budweisers. One round led to another and before long it occurred to me that I was now on my fifth beer. Carter was going on about how his son was married to the Indian rights advocate Russell Means's daughter. He also bragged that he had money, owned a lot of property, and had found a lot of bones. Incredibly, I later learned that it was all true.

Soon the talk turned to dinosaurs. There was plenty of arguing about Sue and the Larsons. Carter seemed to have an answer for everything. Once I told him why I was in town, he said, "If you're going to be doing some digging, you'll probably want to call in the Sacrisons." His comment brought a quick frown from Bob.

Looking at Bob, I said, "What about it? Can we meet them tomorrow?"

"First thing in the morning we'll stop by Stan's and pick him up," he said, rather testily. "Satisfied?"

After one last beer, which rounded out a six-pack, I suggested that we call it a night. Bob drove us back to the Tipperary.

As soon as I entered my room, the phone rang. It was almost midnight and I certainly wasn't expecting to hear from anyone.

"Hi, it's John Carter. I'm downstairs in the lobby, mind if I come up?"

"Uh, sure John," I replied, wondering what he could possibly want at this hour.

There was a loud knock on the door. I let him in and noticed his hands were full. In his left was the partial jawbone of a Duckbill. His right hand held an Indian artifact. Handing them to me one at a time, he said, "Here, these are for you."

Feeling disoriented, both from the drinking and the unexpected gifts, I said, "I don't get it—why are you giving me these?"

Red-faced, Carter said, "I want to apologize for something I said."

"I'm not following you."

While shuffling his feet, he confessed, "When you and Bob left the bar, someone asked who you were and I said you were a queer from San Francisco. But I know you're not. I'd like you to have these as a peace offering—I hope we can be friends."

I looked at the nine-inch-long Duckbill jaw fragment and noticed it was a really nice specimen, easily worth a hundred dollars. Then I examined the artifact, which was a beautifully flaked spearpoint, measuring a full five inches in length. Once again, worth another hundred dollars. I felt guilty accepting these gifts but didn't want to insult John Carter.

"You really don't have to do this. If you didn't tell me what happened, I never would have found out. Besides, who cares what you said? I'm sure it was forgotten the moment you said it."

"Well," said Carter. "I've got to be going. I just didn't want you to think that we're just a bunch of rednecks around here. Hope to see you in town."

CHAPTER EIGHTEEN

The Bonehead Brothers

I awoke at dawn to a remarkable scene outside of my window. The dirty yellow sky was filled with clouds of gunmetal gray trailed by indigo vapors. It was reminiscent of a George Inness painting, the 19th century American master of the atmospheric landscape. Though I wasn't certain whether Inness had painted this part of the country, if he had, this is what it would have looked like.

Once I showered and dressed, I walked down to the town's only restaurant, the Oasis. I had already been warned about the food, but after two bites of my Denver omelet, I knew I should have listened. The Oasis wasn't much on décor, either. A rainbow of plastic fly swatters was fanned-out on a shelf behind the cash register. There was a sign on the wall: *Too bad everyone who knows how to run this country is either driving a cab or hosting a talk radio show.*

A few minutes later, Bob Detrich rolled in. Apparently, he had returned to the No. 3 after dropping me off last night. He looked pretty wasted as he begged the waitress for some black coffee.

"Hey man, you don't look so good."

"Too many beers last night."

"How many did you have?"

Shaking his head, Bob responded, "I hate to tell you that I lost count but it's the truth."

As Bob's scrambled eggs arrived at the table, he reached into his pocket and extracted a fossil claw bone the size of a human hand. The wicked body part belonged to a T. rex.

"What's the deal on the claw?"

"It's from one of the sites where I've uncovered all sorts of rex sign," he said. "We'll be going out there—possibly tomorrow."

As I continued to study the fossil, Bob said, "Hey, maybe you want to buy it? Only $10,000."

It sounded reasonable. He then segued into his financial arrangement with the area's ranchers. After lengthy negotiations, Bob and the county's ranchers association agreed that all proceeds from fossils found on their properties would be split 80/20 in Bob's favor. It made no difference whose land the fossils were found on. All of the money was pooled and divided evenly at the end of the year.

I asked, "Is that a fair deal? 80/20?"

"More than fair. I'm the guy with the white hat! Even if there's only a scrap of bone, and it's sold for only $10, I still make sure they get their $2. If I had to go 50/50, I'd be out of business. Most dealers work 90/10. I'm doing all of the work. Remember, for these guys it's found money."

Bob went on to explain how the ranchers had been burned by fossil hunters on a regular basis. Typically, dealers would ask for verbal permission to search someone's land, promising to share the profits if they found anything. But according to Bob, whenever they found something of value, they'd secretly haul it away. Nine times out of ten, the rancher had no idea that his property had been looted. Over the years, this sort of behavior poisoned ranchers toward fossil collectors. To Bob's credit, he offered a written contract, a foreign concept in one of the last places in the country where a man's word was his bond.

I asked, "How's your arrangement worked out so far?"

"Oh, it's been great—as you'll see later, they're real happy when I show up."

"Is there any downside to your deal?"

Bob thought for a moment and said, "Not really. But I guess if I went too long between finds, some of them might get a little concerned."

This was a valid point. It meant that Bob was under constant pressure to produce, or the ranchers association might not extend his contract when it came up for renewal.

"I'll give you an example of why these guys love me. Last summer I made the biggest score of my career. I found one of the most complete Triceratops skeletons ever discovered—you should have seen the horns! Even better, I found it at an old whore's location."

"I've never heard that expression."

Bob laughed, "Everyone's fucked it! The ranch had been picked over for years. People couldn't believe I found anything, let alone something great!"

"So how'd you do on it?"

"I sold it for $250,000 plus $80,000 for the preparation."

"Not bad," I said. "$330,000 is a lot of money."

"That's true, but after giving the ranchers twenty percent and $10,000 to my brother for helping dig it out, there wasn't much left—especially when you figure I'm still paying someone to do the prep work."

"If I can ask, what did you do with all the money?"

"That's a good question," laughed Bob. "I spent some of it on a new Bobcat—that was $34,000 alone. The rest I've earmarked for erecting my own dinosaur museum here in Buffalo. I mean, this community has been so good to me, I really want to do something for it."

While Bob spoke, he did so with his usual over-the-top enthusiasm. I realized I had never met someone so upbeat.

"How do you do it?" I asked. "Why are you always in such a good mood?"

"It's easy when you know you're winning . . ." Bob continued, "Larson's building a dinosaur museum, and obviously I've been to Triebold's place, but what I'm planning is entirely different."

"How so?"

"Well for one thing, there are too many plastic dinosaurs in the world! I don't believe in casts," he said.

With that Bob handed me back the T. rex claw and became highly animated as he shouted, "It's real—this claw is real! People know it!"

I had to agree with him. In a way, it would be no different than going to the Louvre and viewing a reproduction of the *Mona Lisa*. There's no substitute for feeling the soul of an object, be it a painting or a dinosaur. It all comes down to having an authentic experience.

With that, Bob finished his breakfast and suggested that we head over to the Sacrisons' house. I offered to pay, handing a twenty to the cashier. That's when I noticed a hand-scribbled piece of paper taped to one of those ubiquitous penny trays. It read:

Take a penny

Take two pennies

Take three pennies

Get a job!

With that, we were off. A few moments later, we came to a rather ordinary ranch-style house. The front lawn was littered with leaves and leftover Halloween decorations, including a rotting pumpkin and the remnants of a scarecrow. A rapid knock on the door produced an elderly woman—Mrs. Ruth Sacrison. Her hair was up in curlers; she wore a housecoat and fuzzy slippers.

"Hey there, Bob! Who's your friend?"

"This is Richard Polsky. He's out from California to do some serious dinosaur hunting," he said. "Is Stan home?"

"Yeah, he'll be right out. Why don't you boys have a seat?"

We sat down on an over-stuffed sofa. If I had a nickel for every stain on it, I would have been rich. An overflowing bowl of caramel corn was within easy reach. The venerable Western,

Bonanza, was blaring from an over-sized television. You got the impression the television was on permanently. The sprawling living room contained an overabundance of knick-knacks. It was a kitsch-lover's paradise.

Finally, one-half of the world's most successful Tyrannosaurus rex hunting team appeared. Rubbing the sleep from his eyes, Stan mumbled. "Hey, Bob, how's it going?"

Stan Sacrison just stood there, ignoring me. Not intentionally but because he simply couldn't focus. As he walked toward Bob, the first thing I noticed was that he was wearing a cap, giving the appearance of having slept in it. The cap advertised some sort of farm machinery, its full company name obscured by deep grease stains (or maybe it was months of perspiration). If Stan was positioned in a police line-up, he would have come in just below the six-foot line. Matted sandy blond hair peeked out from around the perimeter of his cap. His blue eyes were clear, yet he hadn't shaved in days. To quote the writer Susan Orlean, Stan's posture resembled a strand of al dente spaghetti.

He lit up a cigarette, went to the kitchen, and emerged with a mug of coffee. At this point, he turned to me and said, "Oh, hi."

"Stan! Stan!" yelled Bob. "Come on, buddy. Let's get going. You can drink that in the truck."

"Sure, Bob. Whatever you say."

Once outside, we made a quick detour to what appeared to be a detached garage. It turned out to be a former one-room schoolhouse from the 1930s, reincarnated as a dinosaur prep lab. Inside were various bones, still clothed in their white plaster field jackets, as they patiently waited their turn to be liberated and put on display. Bob pointed out the skull of the $330,000 Triceratops. He had hired Stan to do the prep work on it.

"See that jacket over there?" said Bob, gesturing toward the corner. "I think we've got a T. rex mandible in it!"

"No you don't," said Stan, finally coming to life.

"The hell I don't!" yelled back Bob.

Then Stan glanced at me and shook his head. Bob immediately picked up on the disparaging gesture and yelled, "Who's the King around here?"

Silence.

"I said, who's the King?"

"You are, Bob," said a deflated Stan.

"Alright. Now that that's settled, let's get going!"

We piled into Bob's pickup, sitting three across. It was becoming obvious that although Stan and his brother had found three T. rexes to none for Bob, the King was still in charge. Mutiny would not be tolerated. I honestly couldn't tell whether Stan was just playing along or if he really acknowledged Bob's leadership.

We drove in silence as the barren prairie whizzed by. About five miles later, a field of giant circular bales of hay broke the monotony. The bales of alfalfa each resembled a long mattress that had been rolled up. Peter Larson referred to them as "Sasquatch bedrolls." As we drove by, their spiral patterns were hypnotic.

"Tell me about the bales of hay—I've never seen bales that weren't rectangular."

"All I know is they're pretty heavy. Each one weighs fifteen, sixteen hundred pounds," volunteered Stan.

I turned to him. "There's something I've been wondering about. Where's your brother, Steven?"

"Oh, he's up in Pierre doing some construction. He should be back in town in a few days. Don't worry, you'll meet him."

"Are you guys close?"

Stan muttered, "He's kind of an asshole."

Stan may have been laconic but he was always to the point.

Bob was silent, driving with a purpose. He was in the zone and concentrating on the business at hand—the Don Hett ranch and its sections of badlands chock full of dinosaur bones.

We arrived at a dirt road that led to a two-story house, surrounded by a low wall made of chunks of petrified wood and local minerals. Bob honked the horn, summoning a barking golden retriever. The front door of the farmhouse swung open and out walked Don Hett. A ray of light ricocheted off his silver and gold rodeo buckle. With his crew cut, ramrod straight posture, and strong masculine presence, he resembled a Marine drill sergeant. Introductions were made and when I shook his outstretched hand the grip was like a vise, the result of a lifetime of ranching.

Hett seemed genuinely glad to see Bob, asking, "Where are you planning to search today?"

"We're going to head over to the rex site," Bob said nonchalantly.

Hett smiled. "You really think it's a T. rex?"

Before Bob answered, he shot Stan a look, making sure there would be no dissension. "Could be!"

Hett continued to smile dreamily, probably allowing himself the guilty pleasure of wondering what it would be like to win the dinosaur lottery.

We hustled back into the pickup's cab and drove over a series of graduated hills. I noticed Bob was careful to stay on the dirt road to avoid damaging the grass. Experience had taught him it was a cattle ranch's most valuable commodity. Soon we came to a two hundred-foot stretch of purplish-gray knolls of clay. Some measured seventy or eighty feet high. It was a textbook outcrop of badlands ripe for fossil-hunting.

We piled out of the vehicle, slowly digesting the eerie majesty of the lunar landscape. The air was full of anticipation as Bob lit up a cigarette and passed one to Stan. They each took a long drag, savoring the moment.

"Hey, Richard why don't you walk around and get acclimated. Who knows, maybe you'll get lucky!"

"Who knows," I echoed back, while gently patting the jacket

pocket that hid the fake T. rex tooth I'd purchased at the Field Museum.

I began walking over small lion paws of hardened cracked clay. The area was completely devoid of plant life, probably due to the acidity of the soil. Before I knew it, I had lost sight of Stan and Bob. Forced to reconnoiter by natural landmarks, I mentally noted a jagged hill as a point of reference. A trail of honey-colored calcite crystals became the breadcrumbs that marked a path. The further I wandered off, the more attuned I became to the topography.

After hiking a half-mile I began to circle back. Within a few hundred yards of the pickup, I decided it was time to get to work. Carefully slipping the "rex tooth" from my pocket, I searched for an appropriate burial spot. I wedged the tooth into a knee-high crevice in the cliff-face, leaving it half-exposed. It had rained the night before, so I wanted to make sure it blended in. I decided to push it in a few inches deeper and dabbed some gray mud on the tooth. *This is going to be good.*

As I finished my subterfuge, visions of Cope and Marsh's "Bone Wars" floated through my head. They would have been proud of my devious tactic.

Walking back I felt a stab of guilt and fear. What if I humiliated Bob and he sent me packing? But it was too late to worry. Besides, the idea was to find out whether Bob was all talk or really knew his stuff.

I found the boys still hanging around the pickup, finishing their second Camel. "Hey, you're not going to believe it, but I think I found something pretty good!" I cried.

Bob and Stan looked at each other.

"What do you think you got? Think it's bone?" queried Stan.

"I don't know, but it could be the tip of a tooth—a big tooth," I said.

Taking the bait, Bob yelled, "Come on—lead the way!"

Despite methodically retracing my steps, I momentarily forgot where I had salted the tooth. Trying not to panic, I luckily spotted a landmark and picked up the trail again. Bob and Stan walked in silence as their eyes darted around, flirting with the land for fossils. Before long, I found the site. "Let's see . . . I know it's here somewhere."

Stan was the first to spot it. He elbowed Bob and pointed. The two amateur paleontologists looked at each other knowingly, then glared back at me.

"Nice cast," said Bob flatly.

It was as if Bob had been expecting me to provoke him. Or maybe somebody had pulled a similar prank on him. Removing the tooth from its constructed home, I handed it to Bob, thinking he might want it as a trophy. I could have sworn he muttered under his breath, "Revenge will be sweet." But I was probably just imagining it.

Stan and Bob pulled out their packs of Camels, tapping out individual cigarettes as they talked. Thunderheads appeared in the distance. The boys finished smoking, then ground out their butts and began walking. There was a spring to Bob's step as he looked over his shoulder and grinned at me.

He had passed the test.

CHAPTER NINETEEN

Stan Does it Again

Many of us, especially boys, spent part of our childhood playing with dinosaurs. It was almost a rite of passage, a universally shared experience. Once in your early teens, the interest in dinosaurs usually fades and you move on to intriguing things like cars, sports, and girls. Yet, guys like Bob Detrich and the Sacrison brothers never lost their enthusiasm for fossils.

That day, while we were out in the field, I addressed the psychology issue with Bob, "So how come you never lost interest in dinosaurs when you grew up?"

He quickly responded, "Who knows? Maybe it's because I still have an imagination. Maybe we become too serious when we get older. Maybe we can no longer fantasize what it must have been like to watch a T. rex terrorize his prey. The whole thing's probably too far out for adults. Kids have an imagination—they accept things. Adults can only deal in reality. That's why they lose interest in dinosaurs."

Bob had surprisingly little to say about his pre-fossil dealing days, but he did mention his first real job—as a ball-bearing salesman—which lasted two years. Modeling also proved unsatisfying. His epiphany came when his stepbrother, Alan, invited him to help dig out Z-rex. This was the same skeleton that Alan eventually sold, used the proceeds to move to Hawaii, and then said adios to the dinosaur business.

With a rare flash of anger, Bob hissed, "I was promised $200,000 on the sale of Z-rex—but only saw half the money!"

"What happened?"

Recovering his equilibrium, he explained, "My brother gave me $100,000. But his partner on the deal, Fred Nuss, refused to pay the other half."

"Why?"

"He was pissed at Alan and I guess he decided to take it out on me."

With the retirement of Alan, Bob took over the Detrich Fossil Company and became its sole proprietor. At the age of 42, he was finally his own boss.

I asked, "Did you go to school?"

Bob's blue eyes flinched. All he could say was "some," and left it at that.

Not wanting to grill him, I went in another direction. "What's the story on Stan?"

With a shrug, he said, "He grew up right here in Buffalo. As a kid he used to wander around a lot—Stan knew all the neighboring ranchers. He found a few fossils and kept at it. The sad thing is that he's never made any real money. I know he studied to be an electrician, but I don't think that went anywhere. Stan's father used to fix televisions, so maybe his mechanical aptitude came from him. If you ask Stan, he'll tell you he's 'a jack of all trades and a master of none.' Anyway, like I said, he seems to have always gotten screwed on the fossils."

"Give me an example."

"Okay. He told me he only got $15,000 for discovering his namesake 'Stan'—the second finest T. rex in existence. The Black Hills Institute paid him that as a finder's fee. He's also gotten $1,000 for every cast of Stan they've sold—I think you're looking at approximately 30 casts."

I thought about it for a moment, "That doesn't sound too bad.

When you think about it, he didn't own the land where Stan was found. If you look at it that way, fifteen grand sounds pretty good. And there's the additional $30,000 from the casts."

"Yeah, I guess so," said Bob.

Just then, the real Stan wandered over.

"What are you guys talking about?"

"You!" I laughed.

Stan had a bemused look on his face, wondering what anyone could possibly find so interesting about his life. That's when I noticed he must have been wearing three or four layers of filthy clothing, each in a different stage of being unbuttoned or unzipped.

"Don't worry, we weren't saying anything bad about you. Bob did mention you saw some money from finding Stan. How did you do on 'Duffy?'"

"Duffy" was Stan's second T. rex discovery. After Stan turned the Black Hills Institute on to it, Peter Larson promptly named it Duffy, in honor of the attorney who defended him in the Sue trial.

In his usual soft-spoken voice, Stan repeated, "How did I do on Duffy? I didn't see anything."

"How come?"

"I don't know—I just didn't. I rarely ever see any money—I must be an idiot. I feel like I lost at least $1 million twice by not making the right deal when I found each T. rex," he said. "It keeps happening to me. But I don't care—it's okay."

"That's not going to happen with us!" yelled Bob.

Stan nodded appreciatively. Then the two of them began marching toward what Bob had described as the first rex site. I fell into line as we walked single file through a narrow passage. When we emerged, I looked up and saw a red tarp, cloaking what I assumed was the site Bob had been referring to.

Once we were upon it, Bob said, "Give me a few minutes to clear the rocks and debris off. Why don't you guys look around."

"Alright," said Stan. As he went into action. I thought it might be instructive to observe his technique. Picking a promising spot, he got down on all fours and carefully scanned the ground. His head weaved from side to side, as if he were sending out sonar waves. Unlike me, he didn't wear sunglasses. Nor did he make sure the sun was directly in front of him. There was no apparent strategy. Stan's approach was purely intuitive.

At first glance, there were bits of bone everywhere. Many of the fragments had been bleached almost white by the sun, typical for bones that had been exposed to the elements for a long time. It was also ironic how the bones reverted to their original color, no different than when they were buried millions of years ago.

I watched Stan continue to work. He never seemed to pick anything up. He ignored pieces of bone that I would have been thrilled to keep.

All of a sudden, Stan stopped and motioned for me to come over. He handed me something brown, about an inch-long, and conical in shape. At first, I couldn't identify it. Then it occurred to me *why* the fossil was conical in shape—it was an ancient pine-cone. Stan explained these cones were from sequoias. As he told it, we were standing in a barren field that had once been a lush forest. Vegetation and wildlife were abundant.

I asked Stan, "Don't you think we should check on Bob and see how he's doing?"

"Nah," he said. "Let Bob have his fun. I know he thinks he's got a rex skull under that tarp but I seriously doubt it."

Out of the corner of my eye, I noticed a smattering of bone. I went over to investigate but none of the pieces had any structural form, so I moved on. That's when I realized Stan had been trailing behind me. It was as if he didn't trust my fossil hunting skills. Having searched for fossils many times in the past, I felt confident in my ability to detect anything of consequence. There was little chance I would overlook something. In fact, it was actually starting to bug me that Stan was sticking so close.

Just as I was about to lodge a complaint, Stan raised his hand.

"Take a look, Richard," he said with a smile. Then he cupped his hands and yelled, "Hey, Bob—get over here!"

Retracing my steps, I got down on my hands and knees where Stan was pointing. I couldn't believe it. Directly in front of me was the tip of a T. rex tooth, *that I literally stepped over*. I didn't know whether to laugh or cry. At first, I thought Stan planted the fake to get even with me. But touching the tooth I saw it was naturally fixed in place.

Bob came charging down the hill, setting off a tiny avalanche with each step. Once his eyes locked onto the tooth he grabbed me and yelled, "There you have it! We've already found a T. rex!"

Stan shook his head and said, "It's just a tooth, for crying out loud."

But sometimes a tooth is enough. Bob immediately seized on it as confirmation that what lay under his tarp was a major rex. Things were heating up. Bob became agitated. "You see that! I know you guys doubted me. Maybe the two of you will finally get it! They don't call me the King for nothing!"

What was so funny was that Stan actually found the tooth—not Bob. But since Bob held the contract for the Hett ranch, the T. rex tooth was found on land he ruled. The ranch was part of his monarchy. Like a subject bringing tribute to his king, Stan was merely rendering unto Bob what was his to begin with.

Regardless of protocol, I congratulated Stan as he handed me the small piece of fossil enamel. I held it in my hand as if it were the Hope diamond. Although the tooth was only around an inch-long you could plainly see the serrations. Stan knew it was a rex tooth and not from another carnivore because of its thickness. Only a Tyrannosaurus rex had teeth this robust. Stan pointed out how hard it was to find a complete rex tooth. For some unknown reason, when one works its way up to the surface, it usually "explodes."

"Come on, let's see if we can find the rest of it," he said, as we began carefully combing the ground. Meanwhile, Bob took off and headed back to his site. As the two of us continued to search, we came across small bits of tooth. Sadly, these splintery fragments would be impossible to glue back together.

"Think there's anything else here? Maybe some other teeth that could be part of Bob's rex?" I suggested.

Lighting a cigarette, Stan stared off into space. "There is no rex—you'll see. It's possible that we'd find another tooth. But it's random. Some T. rex shed his teeth or maybe they just broke off when he was feeding. They're not rare. But I guess they're not common either."

It was starting to get late and rain clouds were rolling in. Calling it a day, we helped Bob replace the tarp, anchoring its perimeter with large pieces of stone. Then we climbed in the pickup and drove back to the farmhouse. Just as Bob had said earlier, he needed to honor his agreement by showing Don Hett our find.

I said, "Hey Bob, what are you going to do with the tooth once you show Don?"

"I guess I'll sell it."

"Well, I'd be interested in buying it," I said.

Bob smiled, "You know I'd just give it to you. But I've got to do the right thing. You understand?"

"Sure I do. But seriously, how much do you want for it?"

"Hmm," pondered Bob. "Didn't you once tell me T. rex teeth brought $1,000 an inch? Well this one's a little over an inch . . ."

The collector in me vanished and the businessman quickly returned. "Come on! That's for a tooth in perfect condition—this is hardly museum quality. I just want it as a remembrance."

I could tell Stan was enjoying the haggling. Deal making was as exotic to him as finding a rex tooth was to me.

Bob said, "Tell you what—let's call it $400." "No way!"

"All right," he said. "What do you want to pay for it?"

"I'll give you $200."

"$250."

"Deal," I laughed.

Stan continued to smile as I looked at him and winked.

When we pulled up to ranch house, Don Hett shouted from the porch. "Any luck?"

"Come on, Don," implored Bob. "Don't I always bring 'em back alive?"

Bob handed him the tooth and said, "Richard offered to buy it for $250."

As he was saying this, I reached for my wallet and discovered I had exact change. I handed Bob two hundreds, two twenties, and a ten. With that, he handed fifty dollars to Hett, a hundred dollar-bill to Stan, and pocketed the other.

"That works for me," said a rather pleased Don Hett. "I think I'll take the wife to dinner."

"Speaking of dinner," I said. "I'm starving. Let's go eat—I'm buying—but any place except the Oasis."

"Fine. Why don't we try the Crooked Creek? It's over in Ludlow, on the way back," said Bob.

We drove home, each lost in his own thoughts, until we saw the restaurant's red neon sign glowing faintly in the distance. As Bob hit his turn signal, an SUV came out of nowhere and tried to run us off the road. I was too shocked to react. With a rush of adrenalin, Bob laid on the horn. The SUV pulled along side and someone gave us the finger. Then Bob started laughing and hooting and I knew it was going to be all right.

"That John Carter's a real asshole!" he yelled.

"Yeah," Stan concurred.

Both vehicles screeched to a halt in front of the Crooked Creek. When John Carter and his friend Ed Smith bailed out, I saw the front seat was filled with trash—predominantly empty Coors cans. Carter insisted we sit together and buy them dinner.

Looking concerned, Bob asked me if that was all right since I had volunteered to pay. Recalling Carter's generous gift of the jawbone from the other night, I agreed.

Carter summoned the waitress and yelled, "Bring me your biggest steak. It's on our Californian friend!"

I looked over the menu. Virtually everything was deep-fried. While we were waiting for our food, the owner stopped by and handed Bob two halves of a fossil skull from an Oreodont, a common sheep-like creature. Its previous owner had run up a bar tab of $80 and used it to cover his debt. Apparently, fossils functioned as an alternative currency in Harding County.

"Want to buy it, Bob?" he asked. "I'll let you steal it for my cost."

Now it was Bob's turn to play businessman. He said, "I would if it weren't split in half," while handing it back.

Once we finished dinner, and I'd paid the hefty check, we unanimously decided it was time to head over to the No. 3. Twenty minutes later, minus Carter and Smith, we stepped into the bar. The regulars instantly greeted Bob and nodded at me. Now that I was "appropriately dressed" in a cap, I felt accepted.

There was a full house because it was "Dart Night." As I was learning, almost every evening had a theme. The No. 3 functioned as more than a bar—it was a community center with alcohol. That night, I looked around and saw fathers and sons bonding over drinks. I also met Eagle Ridge, father of the winsome Turkey. With his sky blue bandana and black Stetson, he was easily the best-dressed rancher I had come across.

Cries of "Good darts!" and "Nice darts!" filled the air. People were organized into co-ed teams and scores were kept. At the end of the year there was a tournament with prizes. What kept the whole scene from being too wholesome was the copious amount of beer being consumed. The jukebox was blaring. A running battle was being waged between country and rock. One guy would drop in a stack of quarters and press all the Hank

Williams buttons. As the songs ran out, his rival would load up on Led Zeppelin.

Being alone, I couldn't help but check out the women. Most were married and zaftig. Then again, almost all of the men were large, or "corn-fed," as I heard one cowboy describe himself.

Swigging a beer, I turned to Bob, "How's the action here? Do you ever meet any single women?"

Over a cacophony of cheering darts players, Bob strained to be heard, "Women? *Here?*"

"You ever think of getting married?" I asked.

"Why buy when you can rent?" he laughed.

"No, seriously," I said.

Turning pensive, he said, "Oh, I don't know. Yeah, maybe. I guess if I met the right 'Paleo' babe . . ."

CHAPTER TWENTY

Fool's Gold

A new day dawned as Bob met me back at the Oasis for breakfast. Unfortunately, this greasy spoon had a monopoly on "fine dining" in Buffalo. The Crooked Creek was over twenty miles away and the local gas station only offered "light-bulb" sandwiches, so named because the doomed sandwich was thrown in a small oven and warmed up by a hot light bulb.

The Oasis's owner, who doubled as the chef, came out of the kitchen to greet us with a pot of Sanka. As much as I enjoyed the small town ambience, I would have given anything for a Starbucks French roast.

As the owner poured us each a cup of weak coffee, I asked Bob, "I was just wondering . . . who was the Fossil King before you inherited the crown?"

"I guess it was my brother, Alan. But he turned out to be a jester!"

"What makes *you* the King?"

"Who else would bring the first T. rex skin ever found to Tucson?" bragged Bob. "Just remember, someday the entire fossil world will acquiesce to my rule!"

Once we finished breakfast, Bob mentioned that Steve Sacrison was finally in town. An hour later, we were at his mother's home, where we found Steve standing in front of the schoolhouse-turned fossil prep lab.

Bob yelled out the window of his pickup, "Steve! How are you, buddy?"

Steve barely resembled his fraternal twin, Stan. At five foot nine, Steve was a good three inches shorter. His brown hair was close-cropped and his beard had been trimmed to symetrical perfection. Gold-rimmed glasses framed his brown eyes. Unlike his brother, he was fastidious, wearing pressed Wrangler jeans, a matching jacket, and a clean cap. Steve projected normality. *How could these two guys be twins—fraternal or otherwise?*

Then Steve yawned and his tobacco-stained teeth made me cringe. So did the words he spoke next: "You think you've got what it takes to find a T. rex? Well let me tell you it's not so easy. You're not going to find anything! You people come out here from parts unknown and think you can take our dinosaurs. Tell you something else—I've been interviewed by every TV station and magazine and all they do is tell lies about us."

Though barely eleven in the morning, Steve reached for a can of beer. "Anybody want a Bud?"

I started laughing, "Isn't it a little early in the day for that?"

"Never too early for Steve!" exclaimed Bob.

Ignoring Steve's earlier belligerence, I said, "Tell me about the T. rex you found named 'Steven.'"

Instead of sharing his story, Steve produced a plastic bag of fossil pinecones. Opening the bag, he handed me one. "Know anybody who'd want to buy these?"

"How much do you want for them?"

"The going rate seems to be fifteen bucks a piece," he explained.

"Let me think about it," I said. "Have you ever made any big deals?"

"I guess if you call getting $30,000 for a Triceratops skull a big deal," bragged Steve, while popping open another beer.

Bob was growing antsy. "Where's Stan? Let's get going!"

"I'll fetch him," said Steve, heading inside the house.

Bob brought me up to speed on Steve. Though considered the more gregarious of the twins, he was a controversial figure around town. While in his early twenties, Steve had married a local girl who was only fifteen. At first, he put all the gossip to rest by being a good provider, totally dedicated to his wife and three children. Now he was divorced and on shaky terms with his kids.

As for his past employment—he'd reputedly worked as a gravedigger—Steve was proficient at operating heavy machinery. He'd helped dig out the T. rex he discovered by bulldozing an access road to the site. Currently, he was making noises about working construction and pouring concrete.

Steve returned with his dog, a black lab named Angel. As he stroked her head, I asked, "Are you going to join us today?"

"No thanks. The fossil market's way down and has been for the last three years. I'm not going out again until things pick up."

Stan appeared disheveled and preoccupied, ignoring his more clean-cut brother. He barely acknowledged Bob and me as we piled into the truck. Our destination was a second alleged rex site that belonged to the local sheriff. According to Bob, the rex claw that he'd offered me for $10,000 was found by a hired hand on the sheriff's property. The lawman was also a part-time rancher and his land was part of the ranchers association. Thus Bob had permission to dig and see what else might turn up. We cruised along at eighty miles an hour, way above the prescribed fifty five. We passed a dead coyote draped over a barbed wire fence, no doubt the victim of a vengeful rancher. They took their share of sheep and lambs. We soon found the turnoff for the sheriff's property. Stan got out of the pickup, opened the gate, and we quickly spotted Bob's idle Bobcat, which marked the site.

Bob pointed out the giant ant mounds that dotted the terrain. Their forms mimicked small volcanoes. Peering down at one, I watched a steady stream of large red ants pour out of a dark hole. They seemed to foam at the entrance, creating a skittering froth of bodies. The whole scene had a hellish quality.

"Pretty weird, huh?" said Bob. "But I'll tell you something, you'd be amazed at the number of micro-fossils that are found on ant hills."

"How so?"

"When the ants are excavating their tunnels, they're constantly bringing pebbles to the surface, including fossils. I've found everything from ancient seeds to tiny mouse jaws," he said. "Here, I'll show you."

"No thanks!"

"Come on—they're not going to hurt you! Tell you what, let's find a nest in the shade. It was cold enough last night for those colonies to remain dormant."

Not wanting to appear wimpy, I followed Bob until we came across a typical eighteen-inch tall hill. Though there were a few sluggish sentinels patrolling, they didn't present a problem to Bob. As he scanned the hill, he began picking up little bits and pieces of fossil. The key was a willingness to get up close and personal. Bob's face was only inches from the surface. Following his lead, I instantly found a miniature-bone, no larger than the letter "B" on this page.

"That's amazing," I said.

"Yes, sir," said Bob. "Ants are some of the best paleontologists around!"

In the distance, I heard the sound of an engine turning over, and spied an eruption of black smoke. It was Stan firing up the Bobcat. Bob instantly ran back to the truck, grabbed a shovel, and headed for the dig. I soon found myself on a large dirt field the size of an Olympic pool. A few days before I arrived in Buffalo, Bob had uncovered some theropod bone in the vicinity.

I yelled to Stan, trying to be heard above the racket. "Bob thinks he's got a T. rex!"

"Bullshit!" yelled back Stan.

Bob overheard our banter and volleyed, "Stan, why are you always so negative?"

Stan ignored him, motioning for Bob to get to work. Over the years, they'd evolved into an efficient team. While Stan used the Bobcat's front blade to gently peel a layer of clay off the surface, Bob stood ready with a shovel to probe for bone. It was a risky approach. If Stan hit bone, there was a good chance he would shatter it with the blade. That's why it was crucial he operate the powerful machine with a feathery touch. I watched as he gently stripped away a section that measured twenty feet long, four feet wide, and *less than an inch thick*. When he was done, Bob anxiously looked for signs of exposed bone.

This process was repeated for over an hour. With each pass by Stan, I heard the ever-searching metallic clang of Bob's shovel. He'd reach down and inevitably discover it was only a rock. After a second hour of digging, I decided to strike out on my own. Right away I spooked a large jackrabbit and was amazed as his outsized hind-legs propelled him rapidly over the tall grasses.

I'd been scouting a formation of fossil-yielding mudstone for half-an-hour when Bob whooped in the distance. I raced back to find him jumping around like a heavyweight boxer with his arms raised in victory, reminding me of the champ, Muhammad Ali.

"Richard, check it out! We've hit bone—it could be a rex skull!"

Stan unhooked his seatbelt harness and emerged from the cab to see what all the commotion was. Bob and I stood there, waiting breathlessly for Stan's verdict.

"Come on, Bob—it's bone all right, but that hardly makes it a rex."

Bob's face grew red. He looked at Stan and yelled, "That's it! I've had it with your negativity! How do you know it's *not* a rex? Huh? How do you know?"

Trying to humor him, Stan began digging with a shovel. As he dug deeper, he started uncovering more bone. The only problem was its fragmentary state. I could only make out a vague oval shape, a far cry from a dinosaur's cranial structure. Stan handed me a piece which he indicated could be dinosaur bone, or just a piece of common fossil pond turtle. As I was starting to learn, the most insulting thing you could say to another bone hunter was you thought he found turtle shell. It was the equivalent of telling a prospector that his nugget was only a piece of shiny iron pyrite, or fool's gold.

Bob stood there stewing. Trying to diffuse the tension, I said, "Hey, maybe it is a rex."

Bob concurred, "We really won't know for sure until it's back at the lab. I say we keep going until we get it out."

With a sigh, Stan brought out a garden trowel and began gently digging around the mystery bone. I joined in, thinking, *It sure looks like a turtle.* This went on for another hour. The three of us circled the spot kneeling like we were gathered around a ceremonial campfire. It was becoming increasingly obvious that there was a lot more bone than we initially thought. The problem was that no one wanted to waste a week or two extracting it if it was insignificant.

You come to understand there's so much fossil bone in the earth, that you can't afford to waste valuable time and resources on anything other than a complete skull, or an articulated skeleton of a non-Duckbill, or a bunch of major wild-card bones you believe to be a new species. As I was discovering, Bob Detrich and the Sacrisons saw themselves as stalking big game—let others hunt the lowly ammonite.

As the day wore down, we finally managed to extract what Bob thought was part of the skull. He then brandished a GPS (Global Positioning System), a hand-held unit resembling a light meter, which allowed him to fix a position where the fossil was found. An orbiting satellite relayed a signal that determined whether your find was on land privately owned or belonging to the BLM (Bureau of Land Management).

The boundaries of most ranches resemble checkerboards. Over

the years, parcels of land were traded between the ranchers and the government. For instance, if Washington wanted to extend a railroad through someone's property, they would make a deal to swap neighboring federal land for the parcel they needed. Maps quickly became outdated. Today, thanks to the Sue case, you need to be certain the land you are given permission to dig on actually belongs to the rancher.

Bob took a reading and explained how the GPS was accurate anywhere between three and thirty feet, depending on how many satellites you were tracking. He found the coordinates of the skull, compared them with a current map, and gave us the thumbs up sign. Whatever he'd found was his to dig up. Despite Bob's unpredictable ways he impressed me with his integrity. Whether it was securing signed contracts, honoring financial arrangements, or determining legal access to fossils, Bob always did the right thing.

The next step was coating the fossil with a plaster jacket. This was a messy but necessary procedure. The idea was to keep the fossil intact until it could be prepared under ideal conditions in the lab. Basically, you tore off wet strips of plaster soaked bandages—the same as a doctor used to set a cast—and wrapped them around the fossil. Once it hardened it was safe to transport. In this case, given the immense weight of our large "mummified" specimen, we used the front-end loader of the Bobcat to lift it into the pickup.

I soon found out that most dinosaur hunters had stacks of these plaster-covered fossils gathering dust in storage. The fossils remained imprisoned. Unless you knew you had something major you saved most finds for a rainy day. Or until you grew too old to collect. The paleontology department at Brigham Young University accumulated so many plaster-encased specimens, that they've managed to fill the entire space under the football stadium bleachers.

Once the truck was loaded, Bob said, "I'll be right back."

"Where you going?" asked Stan.

"Something caught my eye—where you found that tooth," he said, his words trailing off as he rapidly walked away.

Stan and I sat down on a dusty rock outcrop, surveying the canyonland below us. We really didn't say much, content to let the majesty of our natural surroundings do the talking. About forty-five minutes later, Bob appeared from behind a bluff. As he drew closer, I thought how thrilling these last two days had been. If this was the life of a commercial collector—looking for hundred-million-year-old fossils by day and drinking beer by night to some crazy jukebox tunes about life and love—it sure was sweet.

We spied Bob in the distance, striding back toward us. Once he was within ten feet, I could read his facial expression. It was as if he was trying to suppress a grin.

I said, "What's up? Find anything?"

"Nah—false alarm."

Though I was suspicious—he clearly had found something—I decided not to challenge him. We got in the truck and sped back to town, too exhausted to say much of anything. We dropped off Stan and headed back to the Tipperary for hot showers.

Later that evening, Bob said, "I have an idea. Let's do something different tonight—let's go to the No. 3!"

"There's a thought."

Bob's cell phone began to ring. He listened patiently for a minute. Then he seemed to vibrate with pent-up excitement. I overheard a few strands of conversation: "I've done the impossible . . . they don't call me the King for nothing . . . you got that right!"

There was a long pause.

"I'm going to rock the entire dinosaur world! This will even surpass Sue!" said Bob, hanging up with a satisfied smile.

I asked, "Who was that?"

"Oh, just giving an interview. It's part of my job description."

"Come on," I implored. "I overheard the whole thing. What's

the big secret?"

He zipped his forefinger across his lips.

You can't leave me hanging like that!" I cried.

"Sorry, pal, but I have to keep my own counsel. Sometimes being on top can be a real lonely place," he said, suddenly turning solemn.

Later, once we had cleaned up, we found ourselves back at the No. 3. Tonight's theme was "Video Game Night." Groups of husky men huddled over a colorful video game that featured bear hunting. When a grizzly scampered across the screen, you'd let him have it with both barrels. If your aim wasn't true you might hit a cub, which would cost you the game.

Bob and I got in line to try our luck. When our turns came, he proved to be a natural. Not only did Bob obliterate all the bears but he also attained "marksman" status by shooting all the mountain lions. I, on the other hand, stopped the first bear but missed the second badly. My errant shot killed a cub and I was immediately banished to the back of the line.

Four beers and a dozen quarters later, I told Bob I had had enough. He decided to stick around as Steve Sacrison and Angel entered the bar. Steve made eye contact with Bob and it was all over—he was roped into a long night of serious beer drinking. I walked over to say a quick hello to Steve.

"We had a lot of success today. Bob thinks we may have 'caught' a rex."

With a look of disgust, he said to me, "I don't know who's crazier—Bob for his dinosaur fantasies or you for believing him! Just remember, if you want the truth around here, you should talk to me."

The truth? That seemed to be in short supply. What I really wanted to know was what Bob Detrich had found in the field that day.

CHAPTER TWENTY-ONE

Trouble with Identification

After sleeping off a mild hangover, I drove down to the Oasis for my daily share of culinary abuse. Bob was already there, hunched over a cup of lousy coffee. He informed me that he planned to spend the day at the Sacrisons' lab doing prep work. That's when I decided to take a break and visit Peter Larson in Hill City.

As the waitress poured my coffee, I observed a group of senior citizens hunched and crowing around a table playing cards. Over the hacking cough of one of the players, I overheard another say, "Boy, that was quite a scene—that's the most shouting I've heard since Miller's barn caught fire!" The others chuckled in unison.

A waitress appeared to take my order.

"Anything but the Denver omelet," I pleaded.

As she smiled, I asked, "What are those people carrying on about?"

"Oh, you missed it! A few minutes ago, someone from out of town came in and demanded hash browns with his eggs. I told him it was too early—the griddle wasn't hot enough yet. Then he went crazy and started cursing and said he hoped our restaurant was condemned! Can you believe that?"

"Takes all kinds," I said.

Once I finished my pancakes, I began the two-hour drive to Hill City. Though I didn't have a formal appointment with Peter Larson, I felt comfortable enough to drop in. Even if he wasn't available, I wanted to take another look at Stan, the T. rex, that Stan Sacrison had discovered.

At the Black Hills Institute, Peter Larson greeted me with a look of surprise. "What brings you to town?"

"I was up in Buffalo with Bob Detrich and needed to take a break," I said.

Larson grinned, "Bob's a great guy . . . but he has a little trouble with identification."

I just smiled.

"Why don't you come down to the lab with me so I can work while we talk?" he suggested.

I accompanied Larson to a tremendous warehouse that served as a dinosaur assembly station. The building contained hundreds of high-density polyurethane bones. They were stacked on large shelves like auto parts at Pep Boys. There were also shelves crammed with the accompanying molds used to form the bones. When a museum or collector ordered a specific dinosaur, Larson's crew sprung into action. They would select the bones they needed and then attach them one at a time on a steel armature.

Mounting was a time-consuming process. Larson donned his asbestos gloves and dark goggles, then reached for a welding rod. Grabbing a neck vertebrae from a Gorgosaurus (a large meat eater), he used an oxygen/acetylene torch to weld it into place. The vertebrae would eventually become part of the creature's powerful neck. Once he was done, he stepped back from the dinosaur, contemplating the placement of the vertebrae like a sculptor sizing up his work. Not quite satisfied, he motioned to an assistant to bend the neck a little to the left.

"I'm impressed," I said. "It looks so realistic."

"That's the idea," said Larson. "What's on your mind?"

"I'd love to know more about the dinosaur cast business—am I safe to assume that T. rexes are in the greatest demand?"

"Yep, we've probably sold 70 casts of Stan's skull and maybe 30 complete skeletons," he said. "We charge $9,500 for a skull and, as I think I once told you, $100,000 for the whole thing. Almost all of them are sold to institutions, though we did sell one to a private collector. There's also a rental program. You can 'rent a rex' for $10,000 a month."

"That sounds kind of expensive," I said.

"Not really—you can always rent just the skull cast for $1,000."

Though the Black Hills Institute's gift shop generated income, most of their revenue was from the sale of casts and, to a lesser degree, from fossils. "I don't think you realize how much money we have to generate to keep the doors open," said Larson. "You're looking at about $2 million a year."

I asked why he was going in the direction of selling casts. He talked about the difficulty of supplying enough quality original specimens. Then there was the added problem of negotiating leases with ranchers. Larson remarked, "It's risky business. If nothing shows up they get suspicious. These days, dinosaur bones are viewed as natural resources like minerals, oil, and timber. You have to understand that ranchers have hard lives. Remember the Ted Turner debacle?"

"Tell me about it."

"You had all these local ranchers who invested heavily in buffalo herds in the early Nineties. They saw buffalo meat as a profitable 'healthy' alternative to beef. Then, Ted Turner, who has this huge 100,000 acre spread in Montana—plus nearly a million acres elsewhere in America—decided to raise buffalo. Prices collapsed and many ranchers took heavy losses."

As Larson finished his story, we began a tour of the fossil prep lab. He showed me some bones from Duffy that appeared to have faint skin impressions.

"This looks very different from the rex skin Detrich showed me," I said.

"That wasn't rex skin!" said Larson, visibly annoyed. "That was probably some geologic oddity."

"Has anyone ever found a T. rex egg?"

"Not yet," said Larson.

"If one *were* found, any sense of how large it might be?"

He was about to answer when the phone rang. Larson was summoned to another part of the building. "I'll be right back. In the meantime, why don't you talk to Marion Zenker, who runs the office," he suggested.

I walked over to Marion's cluttered desk. She was an older woman with a kindly demeanor, but she had a reputation for being fiercely protective of Larson.

"I was just about to ask Peter how large a T. rex egg would be if one were ever found. Any ideas?"

Marion answered, "Well, we have found theropod eggs, including a nest. They always seemed to lay eggs in pairs of two. So it's a good guess if a rex nest were found, there would be two eggs in it. As for size, the American theropod eggs that have been discovered measured eight to ten inches in length."

"Did they look like large ostrich eggs?" I asked.

"No, they were elongated and more narrow."

"Here's another question," I said. "Peter was telling me that you get $10,000 for a T. rex cast rental. What sort of person or corporation rents a dinosaur?"

"Most of our rentals go to traveling museum shows—not just in America, but Japan, South Korea, and other foreign countries. We've also rented T. rexes to trade shows—there was a home builders show—and television commercials," said Marion.

"Can I ask what product the commercial was for?"

"No."

"Okay, then . . . let's say that I want to rent a T. rex. How does it work?"

"The $10,000 fee is for one month or any part of a month. You also have to take out a separate insurance policy for $100,000 and pay the shipping expenses. The rex measures fourteen by forty feet and weighs 2,400 pounds. It comes in three modular sections and is shipped in three crates. If you need someone to supervise the assembly, we'll fly him out—but that costs extra."

Just then Larson then reappeared. "Come on, I'll show you the warehouse where we store fossils."

Stepping out of the museum we walked down the street to what looked like a giant corrugated tin shed. The sheer number of plaster-jacketed specimens overwhelmed me. Clearly, there were several lifetimes worth of preparatory work. The most interesting were the bones of the largest known sea turtle, a twelve-foot-long monster known as an Archelon. While alive, the entire beast would have weighed three tons.

When we left, I felt dazed. There were too many fossils and not enough time to prepare them. Nor were there enough collectors to buy them. It was depressing. Larson added to my sense of gloom by confessing he was worried about the future of paleontology. "What concerns me is the lack of young people who want to enter the field."

"What do you think's wrong?" I asked.

"No jobs! There's little in the public sector and only three fully-staffed commercial dealers, including us. Hopefully some of the kids who come through here will be turned on to what we're doing."

Heading back to Buffalo, I decided to stop in Belle Fourche. Bob Detrich had mentioned that Walter Stein had quit working for the Rocky Mountain Dinosaur Resource Center and moved to town. According to Bob, he and his wife had opened a ten-room dino-themed motel called the Raptor's Nest Inn. The motel functioned as a home base for Stein, providing him with living accommodations, some income, and plenty of space for a prep lab out back.

I was immediately taken by the originality of the motel's signage. There was a great illustration of a sly raptor luring tourists to spend the night. I walked in and found Stein in the motel's small gift shop holding his young son, William, while arranging a display.

"Polsky?" he said, taking a moment to recognize me.

"Yeah, how are you? Bob Detrich told me you left Triebold to strike out on your own. That was gutsy."

"Well, it was time. I felt good about helping Mike get things up and running. But at that point, I decided I really needed to be my own boss."

Reading between the lines, I sensed it was a matter of money. Stein went on to explain how during the summer he ran dinosaur hunting tours called PaleoAdventures. It was designed with families in mind—part science, part fun. When they returned from a hard day of digging, where better to stay than at the Raptor's Nest Inn?

I spotted a promotional sign that commented on Stein's business ethics: *A T. rex is NOT a lottery ticket! A T. rex is a valuable piece of the puzzle of ancient life and needs to be treated as such.*"

And Stein's website read: "Do you have dinosaurs on your land but you're not sure what to do or who to trust?"

Stepping outside, Stein pointed at a room and said, "Check it out."

Each door was painted in a pastel color. Under the room number was a silver metal cutout of a dinosaur. Each door had a different species. In fact, each room was referred to by name rather than number: the "Mosasaur Room," the "Oviraptor Room," etc. The interiors were decorated with framed dinosaur posters and paleontology-related articles.

Stein looked on with pride. "As soon as I make some money,

I'm really going to fix things up—maybe present a small dinosaur cast in each room."

"That would be cool," I said. "So how's business?"

"It could always be better. But I think we're going to do fine. I'll start selling more expensive fossils in the gift shop," he said. "But the long-range goal is to build my own dinosaur museum here."

With that, we went out to the backyard and his makeshift prep lab. It was obvious that Stein was still setting things up. The air-abrasive unit contained a leg bone from a Stegosaurus that he had recently found. There was also a storage unit bursting with plaster-jacketed finds.

"Your colleagues tell me the fossil market is in the doldrums. The consensus is that it's going to take a pretty outrageous event to shake things up. What do you think?"

Stein nodded. "The pinnacle years for the market were 1993-2001, thanks to *Jurassic Park* and Sue. Since then there hasn't been much going on."

"Bob Detrich keeps insisting that all it would take would be the discovery of a T. rex egg," I said.

Stein's eyes grew large as he responded, "Sure—that might do the trick!"

"And Bob feels confident he's going to be the one to find it," I said.

"Let me ask you something," he countered, while grinning. "How well do you know Bob?"

I finished a soft drink, wished him success, and started driving toward Buffalo. I couldn't help noticing multiple road kills, their red skid marks leaving a variety of Rorschach patterns on the pavement. In the distance, I watched a graceful antelope in full stride clear a fence with ease and travel on at forty miles an hour. When I pulled into Buffalo, it was already dark.

I was welcomed back to the hotel by owner Gene Haivala, who insisted I join him for tonight's football game. The hometown

Harding County Ranchers were in the opening round of the playoffs. Without an NFL franchise, let alone a local college team, high school football was a big deal in Buffalo. There were only nine boys to a team, a necessity based on the small local populations. Still, the stands were packed and the cheering was loud and infectious. The Ranchers were kicking ass. The score grew so lopsided that the game was mercifully called at the end of the third quarter.

When I drove back to the motel, I ran into Bob, who invited me to join him and Stan at the Oasis for some dinner. I glanced at the television suspended from the ceiling. There was a commercial promoting a dino-toy called a "Raptor-robot." I thought, *What are the odds?*

Bob said, "Did you see Pete Larson and Walter Stein today?"

"Yeah, I saw them both."

"What did they have to say for themselves? Did you tell them I have two rexes in the ground?" he asked.

"Well, I did, er, mention that you were on the trail of, er, some pretty major things. But to be honest with you, my comments met with a little skepticism."

Growing exasperated, Bob threw up his hands and cried, "*When will they learn?*" He paused to let his rhetorical question sink in. "I know what we're going to do. After dinner, I'm going to call Bucky Derflinger and invite him to join us tomorrow."

A mischievous smile crept over Stan's face, as he said, "That's a good idea, Bob."

"Damn straight! Then maybe I'll get some respect around here!"

All I could think was this: *who the hell was Bucky Derflinger?*

CHAPTER TWENTY-TWO

The Luck of Bucky

Someone was knocking on my hotel room door. Loudly.

"Come on, Richard," yelled Bob. "Get out of bed—it's eight o'clock already. Let's get going—we've got to go meet Bucky!"

"All right, all right," I yelled back. "I'll take a quick shower and see you downstairs."

"I'll be at the Oasis," said Bob, his voice trailing off as he walked down the hall.

Thirty minutes later, I walked into the restaurant to find Bob half way through his rasher of bacon and scrambled eggs. I sat down and said, "So tell me about Bucky."

"In good time," said Bob. "Just remember that *I'm the one* who's working harder and digging deeper to find the best fossils and sell them cheaper."

I started laughing, "I like that—is that your motto?"

"You bet!"

I then told him about the Black Hills Institute's emphasis on casts and rentals.

"Some are good at making them, I'm good at finding them," bragged Bob.

He was now on a roll and couldn't be stopped. He ranted, "I'll take anybody to the Gobi Desert—I'll out-dig them, I'll out find them, I'll outsell them, and I'll outlast them!"

Though Bob had never been to the Gobi Desert of Mongolia, I was sure he had traveled there in his mind. Unlike myself, who was looking for dinosaurs to determine whether I had done the right thing with my life, Bob equated his search with destiny.

After he calmed down, and I paid the check, we got back into his pickup and drove to the Sacrisons' house. Bob had made arrangements for Bucky Derflinger to meet us there. When we pulled up, Steve was already out front, arguing with Stan.

"Good morning!" yelled Bob.

"What's good about it?" moaned a blatantly hung-over Steve. "Oh, Bucky called—said he was running a little late."

Finally, I couldn't take it any longer and said. "So who's Bucky?"

Stan looked puzzled. Ignoring my inquiry, he said, "Bucky was smart—he did real well on his two T. rexes."

Two?

Just then an older model white Cadillac pulled up. Instantly, the stereotype of a Cadillac owner flashed through my mind. I expected an elderly gentleman to step out of the car. Bucky turned out to be a young kid, only twenty-seven.

As he strode toward us, I was stunned. With his well-cut reddish-blond hair and piercing blue eyes, Bucky Derflinger resembled a young Robert Redford. He moved toward us with the jungle-cat athleticism of a middle linebacker. In fact, he was wearing a hooded blue and gray athletic jersey with the Indianapolis Colts logo—a team he followed fanatically.

"I see you like the Colts," I said. "Peyton Manning's something, isn't he?"

Ignoring me, Bucky ran over to Steve and yelled, "Where's the beer?"

Bob stepped in and said, "Bucky—I want you to meet Richard who's visiting from California. I'm trying to help him get his own T. rex."

Bucky turned, sized me up, and shook my hand firmly.

"Well, then it's a good thing Bob brought me in!" Bucky laughed.

Then, with nervous energy to spare, he began dancing around, "So Bob, when you going to retire so I can wear your crown?"

"Settle down, Bucky," warned Bob. "I'm not ready to relinquish it just yet."

"Where we going today boys? Don Hett's?" asked Bucky.

"That's exactly where we're going," said Bob.

I stepped away from the front porch, allowing the Bonehead Brothers and Bucky to catch up. Bob quietly told me, "You do realize that you're experiencing history, don't you?"

"What do you mean?"

"You're looking at the three dinosaur hunters responsible for finding five of the forty or so known T. rexes."

Doing the math, I knew Stan was credited with two and Steve had one notch on his belt, which meant Bucky, who was still well under thirty, had already discovered two rexes.

"You belong in that group, Bob," I said.

He nodded. "At the end of the day, I'll be standing there reigning above them all."

Then he walked over to the other guys and said, "Why don't we take two trucks—Richard, you ride with Bucky. Steve and Stan, come with me."

Steve groaned, "Nah, I'm not coming—there's no point."

"Fine," said Bob. "Let's get going, Stan."

Bob had procured a second pickup for the occasion. With Bucky behind the wheel, we began the twenty-mile trek to the Hett ranch. The drive provided the perfect opportunity to learn more about Bucky's unlikely story of discovering a pair of T. rexes. When Bucky was eight, his father, who owned a cattle ranch in Faith, bought him a book on dinosaurs. Two days later, his dad took him bone hunting on their land and that was it—Bucky was hooked. As he grew older, his interests broadened to high school football and then he moved on to rodeo. Bucky got married at eighteen and by nineteen he was a father. A year later, while roaming his family's ranch trying to break a horse, he noticed something peculiar protruding from a cliff. It turned out to be a lower jaw, with a few teeth, of a large carnivorous dinosaur. Gathering his tools at home, he dug out the fossil and made the additional discovery of the upper jaw. At the age of twenty, Bucky Derflinger had become the youngest person to ever discover a T. rex.

When he revealed his find, his father became nervous. As a resident of Faith, his dad was more than familiar with Maurice Williams and the Sue imbroglio. Even though the case had been settled at that point, and the Derflinger family held clear title to the land, Bucky's father asked him to keep his find quiet.

Two years later, Bucky finally worked up the nerve to reveal his discovery to the folks at the Black Hills Institute. He set out for Hill City with the jaw sections carefully packed in a jumbo Styrofoam cooler. According to Bucky, upon showing the bones to the Larson brothers, they were champing at the bit to visit his property. At that point, the Larsons and Bucky tag-teamed his father and convinced him it was legal to dig up and sell the T. rex. Peter Larson immediately named it "Bucky." The Institute then began to market the skeleton. The main stumbling block was that they failed to uncover the majority of the skull. Unlike Sue, whose remains were found in a fairly compact area, Bucky's were scattered all over the place. For that reason, it was entirely possible that the skull was still out there.

Although a Japanese museum offered the highest price, they decided to sell it to the Children's Museum of Indianapolis for $1.2 million. (Had the skull been included, they could have added at least a million dollars.) The museum had actively courted Bucky Derflinger. The turning point came when they flew him and his wife to Indianapolis to showcase the potential home for his namesake. Besides, the trip was an excuse to watch his beloved Colts play.

The terms of the deal included future considerations. Bucky agreed that if he discovered any additional bones belonging to the T. rex, he would turn them over to the museum at no additional charge. The agreement ran through the end of 2005. However, Bucky told me he would still honor the deal if anything turned up after that date, including the skull.

Upon signing the contract with the museum, the Black Hills Institute split the fee with Bucky's dad. His father then turned around and gave half of it to his son. Armed with $300,000, Bucky used his winnings to buy a ranch for his own family. In the vicinity of Faith, $300,000 went a long way. His windfall was greeted with a bit of jealousy. The townsfolk began to refer to him as "dinosaur rich."

"That's an amazing story," I commented.

"Yeah, I was really lucky. In fact, I didn't know how lucky I was until I found out that the Indianapolis museum had originally agreed to buy a rex called 'Tinker.'"

"What happened?"

"I don't have the whole story," said Bucky. "But from what I heard, a team from the museum flew out to South Dakota to take a look at the rex, which was still in the ground. They were driven out to the site with Bob Bakker, who was hired to evaluate the dinosaur. If you can believe this, the van they rode in had its windows covered over with cardboard. Obviously, the sellers didn't want them to see where they were going. But when they got out to the site—there was no dinosaur. The would-be sellers claimed they couldn't find it."

"Come on," I said.

"There's more. Tinker is now being held as evidence in a lawsuit. It turned out that it was discovered on land that belonged to the county. The guys who found it dug it up and moved it to private property, claiming that's where it was actually found. But they forgot where they stashed it," concluded Bucky.

"That's pretty crazy," I said.

"Crazy but true."

Bucky then shared stories about life as a rancher. He owned 300 head of Angus steers, considered the finest quality cattle. As Bucky explained it, these were good times. The price of Angus beef had climbed to $1.30 a pound—up from 60 cents a year ago.

I asked him, "Do you eat a lot of beef?"

He looked at me as if I was from another planet. "Every night."

"Doesn't that grow old?"

"What are you talking about? One night we have T-bones, one night beef Stroganoff, another night burgers . . ."

"Don't you ever feel like a piece of salmon?" I asked.

"No, I don't. My family loves beef."

Meanwhile, we noticed that Bob's pickup was slowing down. We watched Stan hop out and open the gate to the Hett ranch. We followed them through and then set out for Bob's first rex site. The four of us made the short hike to the spot covered with the red tarp. We quickly removed the debris that anchored it.

Bucky spoke first. "That's no T. rex!"

Here we go again . . .

Rather than take the bait, Bob responded, "Let's just keep digging and see where it leads us."

We all nodded and began gently scraping dirt away. The ground was wet and my jeans soon became smeared with clay. As we uncovered more bone, Bucky said, "It doesn't look like theropod bone to me . . ."

Once again, Bob kept his cool, refusing to be drawn into a debate. Stan typically didn't say a word, preferring to concentrate on the task at hand. About half an hour later, Bob abruptly left his rex site and returned to where Stan had found the T. rex tooth. Putting two and two together, I sensed it had to do with the mysterious phone conversation I overheard the other day.

Bucky continued to dig away. He was now lying on the ground, preferring to work as closely as possible. At this point, he was using an X-Acto knife blade to shave off clay.

I went over to him and asked, "Any progress?"

"Hard to say," said Bucky, wiping his brow. "It's probably a plant-eater. We really won't know for sure until we find some teeth or a large bone so we can check it for camellate structure."

Stan had wandered off. I spotted him in the distance. The flapping of his green shirt kept him from blending in to the surrounding sage-covered landscape. Occasionally, he would kick at something. It made me recall reading about his casual approach to fossil hunting. He was once quoted in an article as saying, "When I need a rex, I'll go take a poke at it."

Not wanting to arouse suspicion by being gone too long, Bob returned to check on Bucky's progress. Bucky looked up and cried out, "Your Royal Highness, I don't think we've got anything here."

Bob just shrugged and said, rather smugly, "That's okay."

By now, we were ready to call it a day. Bucky needed to return in time for supper with his family. The rest of us drove back to town. Having gotten into the spirit of Buffalo, I insisted we return to the No. 3. Not surprisingly, no one objected.

The bar was jammed. Oil field workers rubbed shoulders with ranchers and sportsmen. There was plenty of talk about deer hunting licenses. Not only was it deer season but it was also pheasant season. That meant the area was crawling with out-of-town hunters, starved for a bit of Great Plains adventure.

If the No. 3 had a theme that evening, it would have been "Lady's Night." There was a disproportionate number of women sipping beers, while catching up on gossip. Judging by all the laughter, there was more going on around town than I originally thought. I was struck by how most of the women were young mothers who had brought their children along. As the moms swapped hilarious stories, the kids ping-ponged from the jukebox to the video games.

For the first time I noticed the bar was decorated with quasi-antiques: rustic farm implements such as yokes, pitchforks, old cone top beer cans (which actually had some value), and even a few lanterns. From what I could see, the attempt at creating some atmosphere was lost on all the regulars. They just wanted their beers served fast and cold.

Bob and I took our seats while Turkey Ridge eyed him from the end of the bar. She was with her strapping husband, who cut a cool Marlboro man figure.

I said to Bob, "Don't even think about it."

He just smiled dreamily, seemingly preoccupied by his day in the field. It was obvious to me that something out of the ordinary had gone down. But what?

I looked at Bob and said, "Are you sure there isn't something you want to tell me?"

Grinning like a hyena, he remained silent.

As Friday rolled around my time in Buffalo was drawing to a close. That particular day began like any other—a stomach-churning breakfast at the Oasis and further outrageous comments from Bob Detrich. We had spent the previous few days digging at the Hett ranch. Every so often, Bob would sneak off to his mystery site, disappearing for hours. Then he'd return and say nothing.

Over a second cup of coffee, Bob finally "fessed" up. "I'm about to unravel a secret that only the earth will reveal."

"What?"

"Congratulations, Richard—you witnessed it!"

"Witnessed what?"

"I think I've got a whole T. rex nesting site with embryonic rex eggs!" he said. By the tone of his voice, it seemed he had even amazed himself.

I was nearly speechless. "You're kidding!"

"I discovered a natural depression in the ground that looks

like it was once intentionally dug out. As I began digging, I came across fine sediment and fossilized plant matter—even some pinecones. Then I hit the mother lode: egg shell, tiny toe bones, claws, and bits of skin attached to a skull!" he crowed.

"You've got to be kidding," I repeated.

"A party's in order!" yelled Bob.

"What did Stan say?"

"Stan doesn't know shit!"

"What did Steve say?"

"Steve doesn't know shit!"

His voice climbing, he screamed, "I'm finding stuff the dinosaur world can't fucking identify! I'm relentless! I'm a hired gun! I'm a fossil mercenary!"

"Bob, Bob, easy—I'm with you, buddy," I said, as the restaurant's patrons stared. "Let's go have a look at it later, before I head home."

"Richard, you know I love you, man. But you're going to have to be patient. This is bigger than both of us. All will be revealed at the right time."

Bob's plan was to display his treasure at the next Tucson show, which was rapidly approaching. If he truly had what he thought he had, he would become the most famous dinosaur hunter alive. The impact of a T. rex nest discovery would catapult him into the fossil world stratosphere. It would also galvanize the market. His clientele would expand exponentially. Museum curators would invite him to speak at symposiums. Fellow dealers would seek his expertise. His legacy would be assured. The King would live forever.

Bob couldn't be constrained, "This is the pinnacle of paleontology. Those I've told are skeptical . . . but I know I'm right. This is it!"

Though a Tyrannosaurs rex egg had not yet been found, eggs from more than 100 other dinosaur species have been uncovered. According to *National Geographic*, since Roy Chapman Andrews's discovery, dinosaur eggs have been found on five continents: Asia (109 sites), Europe (39 sites), North America (37 sites), South America (12 sites), and Africa (2 sites). If you break the locations down further, the majority of eggs have been found in China, Mongolia, India, the United States, and Argentina. The most common species of dinosaur eggs found are Oviraptors and Hadrosaurs (plant-eaters that resemble Duckbills).

The biggest prize of all is an egg with indications of embryonic development. Eggs preserved with tiny bones were even more rare. Naturally, paleontologists were anxious to examine as many of these as possible. The possibility of finding a T. rex egg, let alone one which contained a pre-juvenile skeleton, was more than any of them could hope for. But not Bob Detrich. He was beyond hoping. He believed he had *at least* one.

As I pondered Bob's alleged discovery, the allure of becoming a professional paleontologist grew stronger. This was the sort of action I once dreamed of. I imagined being the one who found the T. rex nest. In the art world, it would be the equivalent of identifying the next great artist—the next Andy Warhol—or discovering a lost Leonardo. Actually, take that back. This was bigger.

CHAPTER TWENTY-THREE

Dino Eggs, Over Easy

Four months later, I was busy making plans to drive to the fossil fair at Tucson. Before leaving for Arizona, I called Bob Detrich at "world headquarters"—Great Bend, Kansas—to see how things were shaping up. Despite a dusting of snow on the ground, he had been out in the field earlier that day, collecting a Hesperornis (a large sea-going bird with teeth).

"Hey, Bob," I said. "How's it going?"

"Richard! Things are great—if I were doing any better it would be illegal!" he raved. "Are you coming to Tucson for the grand unveiling?"

"Of course I am. I'm excited for you." I replied. "But I was wondering . . . is the T. rex nest going to be for sale?"

"You know, I've given a lot of thought to that. What I decided to do is price it at $8.4 million—exactly $100,000 more than Sue."

"Would you take $8.35 million?" I joked.

"Oh, I don't know," he said, in a serious tone. "I'd really have to think about it. Besides, when people see it in person, I really don't think money will be an issue. It's like it says on my business card: 'Best Fossils in the World.' People will always pay for the best!"

"Spoken like the King!" I said. "See you in Arizona."

I arrived in Tucson on a Sunday, just in time for the opening of the two-week long event. Nostalgia gripped me as I walked around my old neighborhood, the El Presidio, revisiting the Rosalia Verdugo House, an 1877 adobe I had owned with my wife. Unfortunately, the new owners decided to leave their mark on the venerable structure with a garish paint job. My former home now resembled a Mexican beauty parlor. After a quesadilla made with Hatch green chilies at the B-Line, I walked over to the Inn Suites Hotel.

Most of the fossil dealers were ensconced there, the action having shifted from the Vagabond. Before meeting Bob, I decided to walk around, taking the temperature of the show. At first glance, prices seemed higher. There were even more exhibitors than I remembered and many of the leading fossil purveyors were emphasizing the sale of casts over original skeletons.

Two years ago, I was struck by the prominence of Moroccan dealers and their fossil wares. Now they dominated the show. All the Moroccans appeared to have the same things for sale: giant trilobites, gargantuan ammonites, and an endless supply of polished orthoceras slabs (creatures with shells that resemble torpedoes). It was absurd. Few looked like they were selling anything. A lot of downcast faces greeted me as I went from room to room.

On a more upbeat note, overall attendance felt strong. There was plenty of media exposure, with large promotional billboards gracing downtown Tucson. This year the official mineral was garnet. Each billboard featured a superb reddish-orange garnet crystal in its natural matrix. If that wasn't enough of an enticement, there was also a free shuttle bus to each motel and outdoor tent. Since the show seems to add a new venue each year, a transportation strategy was essential.

The Inn Suites ballroom housed the two biggest exhibitors, the Black Hills Institute and Triebold Paleontology. Quickly recognizing Mike Triebold, I walked over to re-introduce myself.

"Hey, Mike. I hope you remember me from your cocktail party—you know, for the grand opening of your museum."

"Sure I do. Good to see you again, Richard," he responded warmly. "Did you ever get out into the field to look for that T. rex?"

"Yeah, I got out a few times—even searched Maurice Williams's ranch—but can't say I found anything. For what it's worth, I recently hooked up with Bob Detrich and took another shot at it."

With that confession, Mike's eyes grew large in mock surprise.

"What's the buzz on Bob's T. rex nest?" I asked.

Triebold scrunched his face. "What are you talking about?"

"Didn't Bob tell you that he was bringing the first T. rex nest ever found?"

"That's ridiculous—*no way* it's a nest," he blurted out.

"I don't know," I said, with a lilt in my voice. "Bob sounded pretty confident he could deliver the goods."

"Come on, don't you know by now—everything Bob finds is a T. rex until proven otherwise," said Mike. "By the way, have you seen him? I have a skull that I need to return to him."

As I stood under Triebold Paleontology's newest cast of an imposing Tylosaurus (a fierce marine reptile), I spotted his assistant, Tracie Bennitt. Tracie was a tall woman, with flowing long brown hair, and a ready smile. She approached us holding a leash. When I looked down to see what was on the other end of it, all I saw was a stuffed animal. As she drew closer, I realized that it was a thirty-inch tall stuffed T. rex. The toy was a bright teal with purple spots. Tracie was "frog marching" the faux rex; its jerky motion almost brought it to life.

"Hi, I'm Tracie and this is Sam," she grinned.

"'Sam?' What kind of a name is that for a dinosaur?" I laughed.

"I suppose it's as good as any," she said. "The thing about Sam is that he gets all excited when there are a lot of mammals around."

I decided not to read too much into her comment and kept going.

Henry Galiano was sharing a room with the dinosaur egg expert, Charlie Magovern. Their room space was dominated by an Oviraptor nest, lined with a circle of twenty-nine beautifully prepared eggs. At $35,000 (casts were $2,800), it seemed like a steal. As I looked around the room, I realized nobody was home. Typical of the fair, there was a remarkable degree of trust between the dealers and the public. Thefts were rare.

I bent over to examine a coal-black Chinese trilobite, when Henry walked in.

"Hey, good to see you. Have you looked at our nest yet?" he asked.

"It's great!" I said. "And speaking of nests have you seen Detrich's?"

"Detrich's what?"

"T. rex nest."

Henry looked incredulous. All he could mutter was, "Jesus."

"Do you know where he's supposed to set up?"

"I heard he's over at the Fossil Co-Op," offered Henry.

"Thanks, I'll talk to you later," I said with a wave.

Then he called after me, "You should go see Terry Manning—he's one of the world's leading authorities on dinosaur eggs."

My next stop was a quick check-in with Diana Hensley and Jared Hudson of In the Beginning Fossils. I hadn't talked to them since our last beer at the Rushmore Brewery in Hill City, South Dakota. As I climbed the stairs to their second-floor room, I couldn't help but notice a "Mineral of the Month Club" banner slung over the railing. This month it was azurite, known for its deep blues. The specimen illustrated on the banner was museum quality, prompting me to think, *There's no way this mineral is going to show up in your mailbox for "only $39.95 a month."*

Jared and Diana's room held one of the finest displays of the fair. Unlike most dealers, who tried to cram in as many specimens as possible, they went the minimal route. Utilizing tables covered with black cloths, each fossil was positioned with a generous amount of surrounding space, allowing the specimens to breathe. Though there were only about two dozen fossils for sale, all were sublime.

My eyes quickly locked onto the nicest Oviraptor egg I had ever seen. It had about 95% of the original shell and the prep work was exquisite. Every microscopic "peak and valley" of the egg's textured surface was prominent. At $1,200, it was also the most expensive Oviraptor egg I had come across.

Even though Jared and Diana still worked together, they were no longer a couple. Apparently, the pressure of Jared's extended periods away in the field, along with the financial uncertainties of the fossil business, had taken their toll.

"By the way," I said. "Have you heard anything about Bob Detrich and the T. rex nest he's supposed to bring?"

Jared, who was not the most demonstrative person I had ever met, suddenly perked up and began laughing—hard.

"I take it you're not impressed?"

Even Diana, the epitome of decorum and good manners, started giggling at the preposterous nature of my inquiry. I decided to take Henry's advice and seek out Terry Manning.

In his early sixties, Manning was a short skinny man with eyebrows that slanted downward. He was balding and wore his meager hair combed back. With his scraggily beard he resembled a crazed professor.

Manning offered his hand; the other held a cigarette burned down to the filter.

"Henry tells me you're one of the world's leading experts on dinosaur eggs," I said.

"Oh, I don't know about that," said Manning, with a modest grin and a cockney accent. "I actually refer to myself as a paleo-technician but I occasionally deal a few fossils to pay the bills.

"So how did you get into this field?" I asked.

Using his hand to shield his eyes from the sun, he said, "I suppose I was inspired by the lack of academic knowledge about dinosaur eggs—which dinosaur laid which egg. You can only identify an egg by finding out what's inside it. Only one in a hundred eggs have embryos inside."

As he paused, Manning began to unconsciously slide a Bic lighter back and forth with his other hand. "All I'm interested in is the truth. Not glory or money, not God or superstition. And I might add my theories are always correct."

The more Manning spoke, the more I liked him. "You don't happen to know Bob Detrich, do you?"

Manning bared his teeth. "Detrich? He's barking mad!"

"Have you heard the rumor that he's uncovered a T. rex nest?"

"He's a total nutter. It doesn't compute!"

"Well, why do you think a T. rex egg has never been found?" I asked.

Now Manning was on familiar turf. He began to expound on how most dinosaur eggs that have been discovered came from herd animals. These dinosaurs laid many eggs. It was a numbers game. Large clusters of eggs upped the odds some of the creatures would survive. For Manning's purposes, that also meant improved odds for fossilized eggs.

He also theorized that since large predators tended to be loners, a female T. rex would have gone off on her own to lay her eggs. Chances were she fiercely guarded them. Based on nests found of other meat-eaters, she probably would have laid only two at a time. Once again, a numbers game with a different ratio but equally effective results. A small number of eggs meant a high percentage of survivors. But in this case, few (if any) were preserved as fossils.

"Regardless," I said, "Bob's planning to bring his nest to Tucson. Do you intend to have a look?"

"I wouldn't look based on Detrich's word. I mean, no two ways about it—he's a nice guy. But . . ."

I said, "I've got to tell you, I went on a dig with him out in South Dakota and all the ranchers were amazed and enthused by him. Though I do have to admit, I'm still trying to meet someone who agrees with him."

Manning shook his head, "The only way that would happen is if you found another loony!"

"Just humor me for a minute," I said. "If Bob really has a rex nest, what could it be worth on the open market?"

Manning stood there, deep in thought. It was as if even the possibility of such a discovery was too much to contemplate. His professional lifetime had been consumed by working with dinosaur eggs. Now, faced with even a mere whiff of a T. rex egg's existence, he suddenly found himself overwhelmed with emotion.

Measuring his words carefully, he said, "If he had it and could prove it—which I seriously doubt—any price would be too low."

Pausing again, Manning stated, "It would be absolutely priceless."

CHAPTER TWENTY-FOUR

Waiting on the King

The Gem, Mineral and Fossil Showcase of Tucson was now forty-eight hours old, and there was still no sign of Bob Detrich.

Meanwhile, it was another clear sunny day in Tucson. I had been staying with my former next-door neighbor, Monty Jones, who conveniently lived only a block away from the Inn Suites. Once I passed through the hotel's lobby, I spied a gathering of dealers, sitting poolside. Lush orange trees, whose branches groaned under the weight of their fruit, surrounded the kidney-shaped pool.

Mike Triebold cried out, "Richard, come join us!"

He was seated with his wife, JJ. She ran the store at the Rocky Mountain Dinosaur Resource Center and was here on a buying trip, hoping to stock up on decorative minerals, jewelry, and other natural history-related items. It was obvious that she was Mike's rock, providing stability and moral support. That day, she wore her red hair back; a tight leotard highlighted her curvy figure.

I said to the Triebolds, "You never told me how you got into the fossil business."

JJ fielded the question with her usual good humor, "Everybody always asks us that! When Mike and I first met, I used to be a hair-stylist with a large clientele. I was known as the "Hair Goddess"—seriously! Mike was in the radio broadcasting business."

She paused. "You know we owned eleven radio stations."

"Wait a minute—we only owned a small piece of them!" interrupted Mike, looking like he was going to have a heart attack. That day, he was dressed as a stylish banker, outfitted in a black suit, black shirt with white collars, purple tie, and suspenders.

"So then what happened?" I asked.

Mike said, "I was thirty-six or thirty-seven and bored with my job—bored with my life. I forgot where but I came across Bakker's *The Dinosaur Heresies*. You probably know it—its premise was revolutionary—that dinosaurs were warm-blooded. I had always been interested in dinosaurs and fossil collecting. After reading it something went off in me—all of a sudden I knew what I wanted to do with the rest of my life."

JJ sat there listening patiently. She knew Mike was about to come to the good part of the story.

"So, that night I came home from work and announced to JJ that I quit my job and thought I could make a good living as a fossil dealer," said Mike, grinning away.

"How did you feel about that, JJ?" I asked.

Playing a well-rehearsed part, from having told the story umpteen times, she said, "I broke down and started crying—I cried for two days. I mean, we were parents, we had a mortgage, and my husband quit a steady job—to sell fossils! I thought he'd lost his mind!"

Mike reminisced, "I remember taking all sorts of work on the side to supplement my income. I flew a plane as a crop duster. I worked as an animal control officer . . ."

Then JJ broke in. "But I'll say one thing for Mike. When he makes up his mind to do something—he does it and he does it right."

"Well," I said. "You obviously did something right—I would guess you're the biggest dealer in America—your 'Dinosaur Center' is amazing."

"We've been fortunate," said Mike. "Attendance has exceeded our expectations. However, coming to Tucson is still crucial. I can trace meeting maybe 70%-80% of our biggest customers to this show. You never know who'll wander into your booth."

"So what's hot this year?" I asked.

"I know you're probably sick of hearing this but the dinosaur cast business keeps growing. A well-done copy of a skeleton will look more like the original fossil skeleton than the skeleton itself because you can eliminate the visible metal armature. Besides, you can keep the original safe and use it for study," explained Mike.

"I've asked people this before but is the future originals or casts?"

"Both."

"So what's the biggest factor in selling dinosaur bones?" I asked.

"There are three important factors in selling dinosaurs: big nasty teeth, big nasty claws, and big nasty horns. That's what gives these creatures sex appeal," concluded Mike.

Stroking his perfectly groomed blond beard, he went on, "What the public doesn't realize is how complicated it's become to collect originals. I'll give you an example. A number of years ago, I was out in the field with Henry Galiano. We were looking around and Henry came across a terrific crocodile skull—it was complete, beautifully preserved—worth at least $10,000. But after taking a GPS reading, we realized it was about ten feet over the line—it was on federal land. You find a 'homeless dinosaur' and you still have to deal with it. So we called a high-profile academic in the area—I won't say who—and told him about our find. We figured, better that someone recovers it rather than have it erode away. You know what he told us? He didn't want to deal with the paperwork to get permits from the government! Three years later, I went back to take a look at the croc and sure enough the skull was completely eroded."

It was a scenario that played out repeatedly. Sadly, Mike didn't see how things would ever change. If nothing else, it might make the originals even more valuable in the future.

"Well," said Mike. "Time to get back to work."

I sat alone for a while, enjoying the morning, when the ringing of my cell phone jarred my bliss. It was Rick Dirickson, an art collector from San Francisco.

"Hi, Richard. What are you doing in Tucson?" asked Rick.

"Hunting dinosaurs!" I joked.

"Anything good there?" he asked.

"Let's see . . . the best thing I've seen is an Oviraptor egg," I said.

"Tell me about it," said Rick.

I proceeded to fill him in on dinosaur eggs and their market. When I got to the part about the price of the Oviraptor egg ($1,200), he interrupted, "Why don't you buy it for me?"

"But you haven't even seen it," I cautioned, "Don't worry about it—I trust you," said Rick.

"Let's get the dealer to send you a jpeg. That way, you'll know for sure," I suggested.

Rick concurred and the next thing I knew, I was back at In the Beginning Fossils. When I walked into their room, there were several Asian customers, gesturing and asking prices.

As one of them pointed at a long bone, Diana looked at her former boyfriend and said, "Jared, metatarsal please."

He then handed her what turned out to be a nano-tyrannosaurus bone. A nano-T. rex was either a juvenile T. rex or a completely different species, depending on who you consulted.

While I waited for them to transact their business, I noticed a rather sullen young guy sitting on the sofa, taking it all in. I attempted to introduce myself but was barely acknowledged. I looked him over. His face was distinguished by a longish dark beard and oversize eyeglass frames. Finally he mumbled something about being called "Jack," and that he was a PhD candidate in paleontology.

As I continued to wait for Diana, I became increasingly uncomfortable under his non-yielding glare. Another minute passed and I finally said, "What's your problem? Am I bothering you?"

Jack stood up and said, "I know who you are. You're that guy I heard about who's trying to get his own T. rex."

Shocked that I already had a reputation, I said, "Yeah, so? What's your point?"

"*My point?* It's people like you who cause trouble with the ranchers. People like you could easily screw Jared out of an important collecting site," ranted Jack. "*I don't know why anyone would even want to find a T. rex.* They're boring—finding one would just lead to a lot of grief—it would ruin the next five years of your life. And a lot of other lives, too!"

Diana had just finished up her deal. She must have overheard Jack's last comment. "I agree. If Jared found a T. rex it would totally mess up our lives," she said. "Think about it . . . the time involved in the excavation, dealing with ranchers, preparing it, mounting it, trying to sell it, possible legal entanglements . . . it would just go on and on."

"On a more positive note," I interjected, "I'm friendly with a collector who expressed serious interest in your dinosaur egg. Any chance of shooting a digital photo of it and zipping it over to him?"

Diana said, "Of course. I'll do it right away."

Less than five minutes later my cell phone began to buzz. It was Rick and yes, he definitely wanted me to buy the egg for him. Handing a visibly pleased Diana a check, I noticed the sour look on Jack's face had transformed itself. He was smiling, now that his friends had made a sale.

"Sorry, no hard feelings," said Jack. "I'm on the academic side of the fence and I guess I'm just fed up with people who make it hard for those also interested in the science—like Jared—to make a living."

"Don't worry about it. I know you're just looking out for your buddies," I said. "Do you deal fossils to help pay for grad school?"

"No—I'm a rare coin dealer."

Recalling my youth, I said, "I used to be a coin collector. I liked to go through my Dad's change looking for rare pennies, though I never did find a '1909-SVDB.'"

I had been referring to the prize Lincoln cent, which was so rare that the only way to acquire one was through a coin dealer. A faint grin crossed Jack's face. He reached into his pocket and pulled out a coin encased in a protective plastic holder. Then he handed it to me and said, "Here's my lucky penny." It was a 1909-SVDB in "proof" condition—worth about $3,500. I was stunned.

"You're alright, Jack," I said. Then we shook hands.

I left the room with a neatly wrapped package containing the Oviraptor egg, feeling remorse for not buying it myself.

As I took a shortcut across the motel's courtyard, I bumped into Peter Larson.

"You haven't seen Bob Detrich have you?" asked Larson.

The mystery of Bob's disappearance seemed to deepen by the hour. I moved on and decided to show my purchase to Charlie Magovern. I found him lounging around with Henry on the patio in front of their room. After encouraging Charlie to inspect my egg, I received a hearty approval. He explained that he could look at an egg and tell you who prepared it. A preparator's touch was his signature.

I gazed at Magovern's outrageous dinosaur tee shirt. He had a reputation for collecting them. That day he sported one depicting a psychedelic Stegosaurus. As I continued to admire his shirt I asked Magovern about his background. That's when he revealed how he had started out in life as a ski instructor in Lake Tahoe. The way he described the experience, it sounded like an enviable lifestyle. But eventually it petered out and he found his true calling studying and selling dinosaur eggs.

I said to Magovern, "The Oviraptor nest that Henry showed me is wonderful. I know you're asking $35,000 for it. What do you think the Chinese peasant received for digging it up?"

Considering the question carefully, he said, "The farmer may have gotten $200, not a lot more. He would have sold it to a Chinese dealer, who in turn sold it to a fossil broker in Hong Kong for probably $1,000. That might not seem like much—but it's about two years wages over there."

Magovern continued, "Everything changed in 1996. That's when the Chinese government reclassified dinosaur eggs from "trace fossils," which had no restrictions, to vertebrate fossils, which were illegal to export. The change was triggered in part by Terry Manning's research. I think it was in 1992, when he became the first person to find tiny bones inside eggs. Once he did so it was all over."

"So are those stories about prison sentences for dealing eggs true?" I asked.

"Unfortunately they are. *National Geographic* once sent me to a small village in China to study eggs as they came out of the ground. The whole time I was guarded by a guy being paid fifty cents a day. But I did hear about a Chinese man, with Canadian citizenship, who got caught. I guess he didn't bribe the right person—or maybe someone had it in for him. He stashed a bunch of eggs with some furniture in a container ship. Just as it was leaving for Hong Kong the authorities waved it back to port. The smuggler languished in a jail cell for a year and a half before his trial."

"What was the outcome?" I asked.

"The poor soul got seven years and was relieved to hear it—he thought he'd get life," said Magovern.

"What do you think it is about dinosaur eggs that gets everyone so worked up?" I asked.

"It's all media hype that goes back to the days of Roy Chapman Andrews. When he returned to America after the 1923 expedition, he expected all the interest to focus on the dinosaurs he found. But instead, the newspapers got hung up on the dinosaur eggs and that was it—everyone's been fascinated ever since."

I decided to move on and take a break. I walked back though the courtyard which was now surrounded by mineral sculptures on pedestals. A bevy of collectors looked on as two sculptors filed away, carving soft soapstone. Most were organic abstractions; a few depicted African big game. I stood back taking in the whole scene. The fair was now in full swing. Collectors and dealers scurried around. Cocktails waitresses worked the crowd around the pool. The sun continued to shine. All seemed right with the fossil world.

And Bob Detrich was still missing in action.

CHAPTER TWENTY-FIVE

Burial Stones

ran into Gary Olson and Alan Komrosky, the young dinosaur-hunting duo from Montana. They escorted me to their space, filled with fossils from last summer's labors. A handful of dinosaur toe bones were carefully arranged on the bed. A DVD of the boys digging up specimens ran on a continuous loop. Then some collectors appeared in the room and the partners became distracted. I began watching the beautifully produced DVD, marveling at where technology had taken the fossil business.

When the visitors left, I asked, "Any word from Bob Detrich?"

"Yeah, he just called," said Olson.

My face lit up. "Really—what happened to him?"

"He said his trailer broke down. But he just got it fixed and should be here sometime this afternoon," said Olson.

I was both relieved and delighted to hear about his imminent arrival.

As we talked, Olson popped open a beer and took a slug. Looking self-conscious, he asked, rather meekly, "Want a beer?"

"No thanks—it's not even noon yet."

Reaching for a clock on the dresser, he said, "That can be changed!"

Exiting their room, I decided to hang out a little longer at the hotel and kill some time until Bob arrived. Earlier that day, I had spotted a four-tusk mastodon skull cast on display in the courtyard and decided to investigate.

The dealer responsible for displaying the mastodon was Joe Taylor. Unfamiliar with his reputation, I wandered into his room. I was greeted by a man whose white beard cascaded down his chin and chest for a good twelve inches. Taylor was in his sixties, wore glasses with wire-rimmed frames, a black cowboy hat, and matching black boots. His resumé was lengthy, with an emphasis on his days as a graphic artist. His claim to fame was that he designed the typeface for the soft drink Mr. Pibb.

I introduced myself by inquiring about the mastodon, "Is it for sale?"

Joe Taylor said, "We're just selling casts—for now. But if you want to know more about it, you could either visit the Mt. Blanco Fossil Museum in Texas or look at a copy of my book."

He handed me a soft-cover volume, *Fossil Facts & Fantasies*. I flipped through the pages and quickly discovered his book wasn't so much about dinosaurs, but creationism. Thanking him, I tried to slip out before I got caught up in a discussion. Too late: Taylor was standing in the doorway awaiting my response.

"So, what's your name? Where you from?" asked the gregarious Taylor. Behind him sat a young assistant.

Realizing I was trapped, I figured I might as well get it over with. "You don't really think dinosaurs and humans lived together?" I asked.

"Of course they did—the Bible says so! Have you read the New Testament?"

"No, I haven't," I responded.

"Shame on you."

"Look, what real proof do you have? Not words but hard physical evidence?" I implored.

"All right, I'll give you proof." With that, Taylor handed me a black rock, the size of a football, whose surface was covered with white scratchings. I took a closer look at the engraved marks.

What I saw was intriguing—a primitive line drawing of a hunter spearing a Tyrannosaurus rex.

"Here," said Taylor. "Take a look at another one. They're called burial stones."

This one portrayed an Apatosaurus improbably biting a man who appeared to be screaming.

"So what's the deal?"

"They were drawn by members of the Ica people, from Lima, Peru."

"You mean Inca."

"No, *Ica*. These stones date anywhere from 500 B.C. to 1,500 A.D.—proving man and dinosaur co-existed thousands of years ago," he proclaimed.

"That doesn't prove anything," I said. "These don't even look like real rocks!"

"They're not—they're cast resin reproductions. But if you look at the drawing of the T. rex, you'll notice it has fringes, like a Stegosaurus. But we've found no fossil evidence that rexes had fringes. That means the artist had to have seen one alive."

Taylor went on. "Conquistadors gave some of these burial stones as gifts to the Queen of Spain. That alone proves the rocks are old—no way they can be faked. The only mystery is why they were done. My guess is they were buried with people as memorials to what they did in life."

Switching subjects, I couldn't resist asking, "When Noah assembled the animals on the ark, how come the T. rexes and the other meat-eating dinosaurs didn't destroy all the creatures?"

Beaming with confidence, Taylor said, "That's really easy. The ark itself was 450 feet-long—two football fields. God only let juvenile rexes on—they weren't ferocious yet. He made sure the ark was dark—added all this white noise—then cooled down the temperature so all the animals hibernated while it rained for 40 days and 40 nights. Everything else drowned. All of the creatures remained on board for a year-and-a-half."

His seated assistant broke in, "150 days."

Nodding, Taylor said, "All right, go with that."

Reeling from sensory overload, I thanked Taylor for the education and asked a parting question: "Do you think it's possible to find an actual T. rex egg?"

"Sure, why not?" said Taylor. Finally, I had found someone who agreed with Bob Detrich.

Leaving his room, I ran into Henry. He looked frantic. "Richard," he said. "I need a favor. Can you give me a quick lift over to Radio Shack—I need a new battery for my cell phone."

I agreed to help him out and we soon arrived at the electronics chain store. While Henry was searching for a replacement battery, I saw a Raptor-robot toy. It was the same one I viewed on television during dinner at the Oasis in Buffalo. Grabbing the joystick, I brought the reptile to life, watching it stagger forward and snap its jaws at an imaginary foe.

Henry found the appropriate battery and we were on our way. On the drive back, I said, "I heard Bob's supposed to get into town soon. I don't know about you but I'm psyched to see the nest."

After uttering the words, I wasn't sure if I really believed them. The mounting doubt of Bob's peers was wearing me down.

Henry confirmed my fears when he looked me in the eye and said, "There isn't going to be any nest."

Dropping him back at the Inn Suites, I continued on to the Fossil Co-Op. My timing was perfect. I spotted Bob unpacking his trailer.

"Bob!" I yelled from twenty feet. "You made it!"

"I did!" he yelled back.

I walked over and we embraced.

"So you got it? You got the nest? Everyone's been waiting for you—there are a lot of skeptics," I warned.

Bob just stood there exuding confidence. On the other hand, he looked exhausted by the long drive from Kansas and the ensuing delays.

"They're all jealous but I've got the proof right here," he said slapping the metal of his gleaming white trailer. The trailer was a twenty-footer. On its side, the words "Fossil King," along with a line drawing of a rex skull, were neatly stenciled in blue.

"I'm not even going to deal with it today," he continued. "I just want to grab a shower and have a few beers."

"Tell you what," I said. "I'm planning to take Mike Triebold and Tracie to dinner tonight. Why don't you join us? I'll pick you up at seven."

"Alrighty," said Bob. "See you at seven."

Two hours later, with Mike and Tracie already in my car, Bob climbed in and we headed over to Barrio for dinner. Everyone knew the hot topic was Bob's T. rex nest, but no one wanted to bring it up. Not even Bob.

At one point, Tracie asked me, "Do you know of a potential buyer for some Charles Knight paintings? They're asking $875,000 for a group of nine."

Knight was arguably the greatest dinosaur painter in history. "Sounds like a pretty good value."

"Oh, I should probably tell you the paintings are all of prehistoric mammals," said Tracie.

Now I knew why the price was low. Mammals just didn't have the same panache as dinosaurs.

Mike asked Bob, "Where you staying?"

In between wolfing down bites of food, Bob managed to catch his breath. "Just down the street at, you know, one of those funky old motels from the Forties. I got a good deal—$219, including tax."

I said, "Hmm. I guess that's not too bad for a night considering the town is packed for the show."

Bob looked at me with surprise, "Not for a night—for a week!"

Everyone around the table laughed. As we finished up our meal, plans were made for getting together the next day. After letting Mike and Tracie off I began to circle back to where Bob was staying. When we arrived at his motel, I marveled at the old neon sign, whose blue argon gas-filled tubes glowed brightly, beckoning weary travelers. The graphics were equally impressive; two Mexicans, wearing serapes and sombreros, taking a nap under a saguaro. Their forms served as bookends for the words *La Siesta Motel–Refrigerated*.

As I said goodnight, Bob offered a parting comment, "Be safe, Richard. Don't let anything get you." I thought it was an odd remark. Maybe he was getting too emotionally involved with the dinosaurs. As I drove back to Monty's, I felt the uncanny presence of something in the car. Something rather spooky. When I came to a stoplight, I turned around and looked at the back seat but saw nothing. I was becoming unnerved.

I pulled into Monty's driveway. As I reached over to put away a CD in the glove box, I caught a glimpse of something in the shadows, peeking out from under the floor mat. In the dim light it appeared to be long, narrow, and sharp like a dagger.

I shutoff the engine, determined to get to the bottom of the enigma. Then I got out a flashlight from the trunk, opened the passenger-side door, and finally saw what was hiding under the carpeted mat. It was the fake T. rex tooth I'd once planted in the dirt.

Bob had his revenge.

CHAPTER TWENTY-SIX

Auction Fever

Tonight was the big night. Whether you dealt in lowly crinoids or prestigious meat-eating dinosaurs, no one wanted to miss the annual gathering of the Association of Applied Paleontological Sciences (AAPS). This was the event that united the faithful of the "fossilocracy." At seven o'clock sharp, the meeting would be called to order, with business conducted over a buffet dinner. Following the election of new officers, the members would be ready to let the good times roll. It was auction time.

Against this backdrop of anticipation, I had my morning coffee with Mike Triebold and George Winters, secretary of the AAPS. Probably in his mid-fifties, Winters was ironically not a fossil collector. He simply enjoyed the scene and the camaraderie. Thanks to his organizational skills and joie de vivre, he was a valued member of the club. Winters asked, "Have you ever attended one of our meetings before?"

"Actually, I did. But it must have been five or six years ago. All I remember was a poolside barbecue with a keg of beer—and everybody was pretty wasted!"

"That sounds about right," laughed Winters. Adjusting the brim of his green canvas bush hat, he turned to Mike. "Remember the famous snail auction?"

"Oh, right, I forgot all about that."

"What happened?" I asked.

Mike began laughing as he struggled to get the words out. "The auctioneer—I think it was Pete—says, 'Now we have this beautiful Turritella!'"

I already knew that a Turritella was an extremely common variety of fossil snail. It was small, growing to a length of perhaps two inches, and resembled a spiral corkscrew. Turritellas were so abundant that they were worth maybe fifty-cents—on a good day.

Mike continued, "So Pete starts the bidding at a quarter and Fred Nuss buys it for seven dollars. About ten lots later, he donates it back to the sale and Pete auctions it off again. This time it brings twenty dollars. The buyer takes it, throws it in the pool, and some little kid jumps in and fishes it out. Then someone in the audience yells, 'Sell it again! Sell it again!' I think we wound up reselling it five times. People were so drunk, that the bidding got up to several hundred dollars!"

"I'm impressed," I said. "Do you think anything like that will happen tonight?"

"Who knows," said Winters. "With this crew anything's possible."

"I know we have one rare item," said Mike, growing serious. "When Edward Cope was collecting [mid-19th century], he also owned a mining company that issued shares of stock. We managed to procure an actual stock certificate. It has an engraved illustration and it's signed by Cope—should bring a good price."

I said, "That sounds pretty cool. Besides the Turritella, have you ever auctioned off anything else ridiculous, like a coprolite?"

Mike thought about it. "Did you know that during the 'Bone Wars,' O.C. Marsh found the first dinosaur dung and as a jab at his rival named it after Cope? That's where the name coprolite comes from."

Though I wasn't sure if it was true, I smiled. "So do you have a coprolite for tonight?"

Winters laughed, "No. But I just had breakfast and could

produce one for you in a few minutes."

Before I could think of a witty response, Neal Larson stopped by our table.

"Ready for tonight?" asked Mike.

"Yeah—I wonder who's going to get the lab coat?" said Larson.

He was referring to an auction item that had become a tradition. Years ago, someone donated a white lab coat that had been signed by virtually everyone who matters in paleontology—Jack Horner, Bob Bakker, Ken Carpenter, Phil Currie, Mark Norell, and many others. Bakker even drew a Diplodocus on it with a green felt tip pen. Over the years it gathered more signatures and illustrations. Whoever bought the lab coat was entitled to keep it for one year—until the next meeting when it was auctioned off all over again. It was considered an honor to "buy" it and was always the high point of each year's sale.

As Neal Larson departed, Bob Carroll appeared at our table. Carroll was the proprietor of Black Cat Mountain Trilobites. A show veteran and one of the good guys in the business, he could always be counted on for a generous donation to the annual auction. This year's gift was no exception—a rare trilobite from his quarry in Oklahoma.

I asked Carroll, "What do you think of all the Moroccan trilobites at the show? I've never seen so many trilobites in my life."

Carroll smirked. "There are so many Moroccan fossils here in Tucson that you can feel the planet tip to one side. Why don't you stop by after breakfast and I'll show you a few things." With that he handed me a cap emblazoned with his company's logo, an exotic spiny trilobite.

Thanking him, I said I'd come by within the hour. As I ordered a bagel the talk turned to Bob's T. rex nest. Without prompting, George Winters weighed in. "Bob just sees things. If he were any younger you could blame it on smoking pot. He's a little like Vito—with the biggest shark teeth."

I finished up my coffee and told them I'd see them later at the auction. But first I wanted to see Bob Detrich, to preview the nest. With that in mind I called him on his cell. After a few rings, he answered, "Fossil King!"

"Hey, it's Richard. Where are you?"

"I'm outside Henry's room—come on over."

I crossed the grass courtyard to Henry's and found Bob enjoying a cigarette. While we were talking, Peter Larson appeared and said, "Bob, I'd like to stop by your space and see what you've got."

"That'd be fine, Peter. Come by anytime."

Despite the casual nature of the fossil business, Peter insisted they firm something up. "How about if I drop by tomorrow morning at ten?"

"Okay," said Bob. "I'll see you then."

Larson walked away. A few seconds later, Bob said, "Did you see that? Peter Larson *came to me* to make an appointment." With evident pride, he continued, "Now maybe you're starting to understand how things work around here!"

"I think I'm finally getting it," I said. "Can I come over later to see the nest?"

"You're welcome to, Richard—just as soon as I'm set up. I've got a lot to unpack—better give me the rest of the day. Don't worry, I'll catch up with you tonight."

Not sure if he was stalling, I decided to give him the benefit of the doubt.

Bob Carroll's operation was so successful that he could afford to occupy two rooms. I had heard earlier that he had brought eighty-five trilobites to the show and sold virtually all of them. Prices ran from $750 all the way up to $8,500.

Black Cat Mountain Trilobites carried a special cachet. On the back of each specimen was a rubber-stamped black cat. The key to the uncommon beauty of the trilobites was their mineral composition—translucent dark tan calcite on a cream limestone matrix. They are so life-like that you expect them to start inching away.

But such quality didn't come easy. During the hot summer months, Carroll worked seven days a week quarrying trilobites. When he found one, it was always in a raw state, needing five to twenty-four hours of preparation. As winter rolled around and it became too cold to collect, Carroll turned his attention to exposing the fossils to their best advantage—he was a nonpareil preparator.

Wearing the cap he'd given me earlier, I entered his room to a backslapping welcome. Carroll immediately yelled out, "Come on in—take a seat!"

Carroll was at least six-feet tall, in his early fifties, and couldn't have been friendlier. He was also wearing one of his signature hats and a matching tee shirt, along with a leather vest, jeans, and cowboy boots. Besides a bunch of empty trays that once held trilobites, there were also two attractive women in the room.

Trying not to get distracted, I asked, "How do you do it? The show just opened and you've already sold everything."

With typical modesty, he said, "Well, there's more to it than meets the eye. Over the years I've built up a following. Got a bunch of hungry collectors who contact me ahead of time, putting reserves on different trilobites. Almost everything is spoken for before the fair even opens."

"Then what do you do for the rest of the two weeks?" I asked.

Hugging his blond wife, he smiled, "Are you kidding? I get to spend time with Linda! We love it here in Tucson—it's nice to be away from those Oklahoma winters."

Linda smiled warmly at Bob. They met during the seventies at one of the first Tucson shows. She was working for a jeweler who occupied a neighboring room. They started talking and by the end of the show were a couple. Back then, Linda called Indiana home. Bob was living in Alaska and racked up 60,000 frequent flier miles while courting her.

With his arm around Linda, he said, "I love my wife—I hope you're as lucky. By the way, are you single?"

"I am now," I laughed nervously.

"Why don't you sit next to my sister-in-law, Kathleen?" he grinned. With that, he grabbed her and playfully positioned her next to me on the bed.

Blushing, Kathleen just looked at me—half-intrigued, half-embarrassed. About forty, she was exceptionally curvy, with flowing curly hair, and nice cheekbones. She was dressed from top to bottom in a black Danskin.

Then Bob took Linda's hand. "We're going to leave now. I'm locking the door and I'm not letting you out until you have a date!"

I just stared at Kathleen in amazement. The whole thing was outrageous. I guess the Carrolls thought if it could happen to them . . .

Kathleen and I began talking. Though she had only a passing interest in fossils, she was a good sport. On top of that it turned out she was from the Bay Area. We quickly agreed to sit together at that night's dinner.

Meanwhile, I couldn't get Bob's T. rex nest out of my mind, hoping he could produce it and not destroy his credibility. Maybe I worried too much. Despite all the teasing from his colleagues, I sensed that deep down inside many of them admired Bob. Not for his ability to find dinosaurs but for his passion. His unabashed joy added another dimension to their profession. More than anyone, he was a true believer in the power of fossils to transform people's lives.

Putting aside my worries about Bob and the hustle and bustle of the fossil world, I drove out to Saguaro National Park. Forty minutes later, I arrived at the park's Visitors Center and saw thousands of cacti spreading their arms, welcoming me. It was a glorious sight. Each succulent's configuration was unique, with its own personality. No wonder everyone referred to them in anthropomorphic terms. Within an hour I felt refreshed.

Back at Monty's place, I changed for dinner and headed to the Arizona Plaza Hotel. Though it was out of business, AAPS had convinced them to rent out their ballroom. Upon entering, you were handed a ticket for the door prize drawing. This year it was an ammonite from Madagascar, worth sixty-dollars. Everyone's next stop was the buffet table. There had been some grumbling about the "exorbitant" fifteen-dollar-a-person charge, despite an overabundance of pasta with meatballs, caesar salad, and garlic bread.

As the room quickly filled up, I counted approximately 150 members and spouses seated around twenty circular tables. No one had dressed up for the affair. I tried to liven things up by wearing my dinosaur tie from the American Museum of Natural History, depicting a silver T. rex on a background of black silk. Surprisingly, I didn't receive a single compliment on it. Instead, a man wearing a bear claw necklace got all the attention.

During dinner, Mike Triebold, the club's president, stood up to read the minutes from last year's meeting. Members actually paid attention. The only distraction was an endless stream of people thronging the cash bar. A moment later, Bob Carroll's sister-in-law Kathleen appeared with a vodka and tonic in hand. She was even more attractive than I remembered.

Genuinely pleased to see her, I said, "Hi there, glad you could make it."

Taking it all in, Kathleen remarked, "What do you think? This is pretty fun already!" Then she said, "Can I buy you a drink?"

"Sure."

Kathleen got in the bar line again and soon returned with not only a beer for me but another vodka and tonic for herself. I didn't give it much thought as I watched her quickly down her second drink.

Mike finished reading the announcements. Then it was on to the election of new officers. Ballots were passed out, votes were instantly tabulated, and a new cabinet was announced. The last order of business was the awarding of the "Sternberg Medal," named for commercial paleontologist Charles Sternberg. This was an honor bestowed on a member for life-long service to the fossil community. This year's winner, an elderly gentleman who approached the podium with the help of a cane, appeared overwhelmed. Apparently the recipient was a sentimental favorite as raucous applause greeted his selection. Tears ran down his cheeks as the medallion was placed around his neck.

While all this was going on, members periodically rose from their seats to examine a long table, crammed with 100 items to be auctioned off. They ranged from fossils—the Black Hills Institute had donated a handsome palm-size turtle—to casts of teeth and claws. There were also plenty of tee shirts, hats, and posters.

Mike summoned Neal Larson to the front of the room. Larson's auctioneering skill was evident as he opened the bidding on the first lot, a fossil shrimp on limestone. Plenty of hands shot into the air including mine.

"I have $40 for this incredible crustacean—who'll give me $50?" asked Larson.

I yelled out, "Fifty!"

Kathleen winked at me. My plans to own the shrimp were momentarily dashed as the bidding climbed to $60, then $70, then $80.

"Ninety!" I cried out.

I had set a limit of $100. Despite being a veteran of high-ticket contemporary art auctions at Sotheby's and Christie's, my pursuit of the fossil shrimp took on the same urgency. Whether the item was big or small, you always wanted to go home a winner.

"Come on people!" Larson implored, "This is a great specimen—

beautifully prepared. Who'll say $100?"

It looked like I was going to get it. The bidding had stalled.

"$90 once, twice . . . I have $100!" cried Larson.

"$110!" I yelled. So much for willpower.

"I have $120," barked Larson.

That was enough—I was out. With competitive fervor, the bids continued to jump in ten-dollar increments, finally cresting at $180. The specimen may have been worth $150, but people intentionally over-bid, knowing it went to a good cause. All the money raised that evening was earmarked for a scholarship fund. Each year a cash stipend was given to a promising paleontology student.

"How about another drink?" asked Kathleen, with glassy eyes.

"Sure. Let me buy this round."

When I returned with her third vodka, she drank it in two chugs. *What have I gotten myself into?* I thought.

Item after item found buyers: belt buckles, fossil fish, Paleo-Bond glue, and other donations. Then the stock certificate signed by Edward Cope made its way to the block.

Neal Larson yelled out, "How much am I offered for this vintage certificate from the Sierra Apache Mining Company? Come on, people—this is signed by Edward Drinker Cope." He annunciated each name, first, middle, and last, as if he were royalty—which Cope was in the fossil world. A forest of hands appeared as the bidding began at $50 and soon topped $300. At one point, Mike and JJ Triebold accidentally bid against each other, with JJ finally prevailing. The coveted piece of history brought $350.

Next, it was time for the signed lab coat. Last year's purchaser zipped around modeling it, eliciting whoops and shouts. The hard-drinking crowd was feeling it. Then it was off to the races. Bids were fired in rapid staccato. There were lots of laughs as a woman stopped the bidding to try it on. Larson obliged her.

The auction resumed with the winning bid coming in at $325, bringing a hug from the under-bidder. The buyer wore it proudly for the rest of the evening.

There were only a handful of items left to go. One of the last lots was a group of five dinosaur tee shirts. The bidding opened at $10, but there were no takers.

Larson urged the crowd on, "Come on people. It's for a good cause!"

With a wild gleam in her eyes, Kathleen looked at me and said, "I'll sell those shirts—watch this!"

Before I knew it she was at the front of the room. Without hesitating she pulled off her top. To say she was well-endowed would have been an understatement. Grabbing a shirt from a startled Larson, she quickly put it on and said, "Now the bidding can start!"

Kathleen began strutting her stuff to wild cheers from the male members of the audience. As she pranced around like a stripper, several wives expressed their disgust, but the men got excited and began bidding. By the time Kathleen's performance was over all five tee shirts were sold.

Mission accomplished, a flushed Kathleen took her seat. "What did you think of *that?*"

"Congratulations! You just made the club an extra seventy dollars!" I laughed. All eyes were on me wondering who was this wild woman I'd brought to dinner.

As the festivities wound down, people began to drift out, but I remained with Kathleen, basking in the afterglow of warmth and humor. Though most of the club's members were friendly rivals, they were a tight-knit bunch. The collective fossil community genuinely enjoyed itself. Upon reflection, I realized that as daily life in our country accelerates, these guys were going in the other direction. By digging for clues about ancient life they were returning to the past. And for most members that suited them just fine.

CHAPTER TWENTY-SEVEN

Deliverance

awoke early filled with anticipation. Today was the day Bob Detrich presented his alleged T. rex nest to the fossil community. Thumbs up or thumbs down? If the find turned out to be historical, I could brag that I was part of that expedition. As Bob said, "You witnessed it!" While it wasn't quite as good as finding my own T. rex, it was still something big.

Bob had generously offered to let me sit in on his meeting with Peter Larson. But I had a better idea. Arriving an hour earlier at the Fossil Co-Op, I found Bob's designated space. All I saw were two plaster field jackets. The smaller of the two rested on the concrete floor. It might have measured two feet square. The name "Gumbo" was painted on its side in crude black letters. I had already heard from Bob that it contained the world's first juvenile Triceratops skull.

The other plaster jacket was bulky and heavy. It lay on top of a wooden pallet. The jacket measured five feet long, four feet across, and three feet high. In this case, "T. rex," was lettered on its side. I got closer and noticed the top of the jacket had been cut off, exposing bare rock. It was as if a section of cliff face had been chopped out and encased in plaster. The rock itself was a grayish brown sandstone from the Hell Creek formation—no fossils were visible.

I was flabbergasted. You would have thought with so much at stake, Bob would have done some serious preparatory work. If I didn't know him better, I would have believed he was purposely thumbing his nose at his colleagues. It was like saying, *I've delivered a T. rex nest—you want me to prep it, too?*

This scenario made me question the dinosaur business as a profession. It wasn't fair to lump the rest of the field in with Bob Detrich, but it reminded me that the fossil market is unregulated—anything goes. Without a governing entity, there was no authentication board to vet Bob's find and render an opinion. In some ways, it was little different than the art market.

I peered inside the plaster jacket. Stretching my imagination as far as a piece of Silly Putty, I could not detect a single indication of prehistoric life. *This is crazy.* Finally, in the lower left hand corner, I saw a faint black area that might or might not be bone. But there was no form to it. Nor was there carbonized plant matter, pinecones, or other nesting material, let alone eggshell. All I could think was, *Bob's in trouble.*

Totally perplexed, I departed and drove back to the Inn Suites. I soon ran into Gary Olson. He said, "You don't look so good. What's wrong?"

"No, no, I'm fine," I said. "I just came from the Co-Op to check out Bob's nest—and didn't see anything."

Olson snickered, "You're not the only one."

"You mean you've already seen it?"

"Yeah, I snuck a peek last night right before the auction," he said.

"What's your take on all this?" I asked.

Olson shrugged. "Did you notice all the loose material on top of the main mass of rock? It's typical Detrich. He'll show you something, then hand you a knife and invite you to dig a little. Eventually it becomes so messed up that you can't see anything. Then you can't deny there was something once there."

"You're kidding?"

"Well," said Olson. "I may be exaggerating a little, but Bob's m.o. is to create a mystery that no one can solve."

As I walked away, I looked for Mike Triebold, seeking his perspective. I found him at his booth typing invoices on a laptop.

"What's the matter, Richard? You look like you just saw a ghost!" he laughed.

"I guess I did, after a fashion. You didn't happen to see Bob's T. rex nest yet, did you?"

Mike confessed, "Yeah, I couldn't resist stealing a look at it . . ."

"And?"

"I couldn't see a damn thing."

This was getting weirder by the minute. Hoping a visit with Henry Galiano could restore my sense of reason, I found him in his room, finishing up a phone conversation. As I glanced in a display case, I observed a few fossils were missing from the day before. Business was good.

"Hi, buddy," I said.

"What's up?"

"Do me a favor and run over to the Co-Op with me. I want you to take a quick look at Bob's T. rex nest," I said.

Henry shook his head, "Sorry Richard, I really don't have time for this. I've got Dallas Evans from the Children's Museum of Indianapolis coming over in an hour."

"Come on—it's right around the corner. I'll have you back in twenty minutes."

"I really don't have time . . ."

"You owe me for wasting two hours driving you to Radio Shack for that battery."

Henry climbed into my car. We arrived at the Fossil Co-Op and quickly made our way to Bob's space. Henry peered inside the plaster jacket. Then he put his glasses on. He looked hard. Then he picked up a few fragments of rock, scanning them for signs of something—anything. You could tell he wanted to give Bob every chance of succeeding.

Finally, Henry spoke. "I'm speechless," was all he could manage.

"Come on. Say something."

"It's sad," said Henry.

As we drove back I was beside myself. While I had to admit enjoying all the controversy, I wanted Bob to be right. I didn't want to see him become the laughing stock of the fossil world. This was turning out badly.

I mentioned to Henry that Peter Larson would be over shortly to have a look. As one of the leading Tyrannosaurus rex experts in the world, his opinion would be crucial.

I dropped Henry off. Then my cell phone rang and sure enough it was Bob.

"Hey there, I just got a call from Pete Larson and he's going to be a little late. Want to grab an early lunch?" he asked.

"Let's do it—I'm on my way."

When I picked Bob up, he couldn't have been happier. It was as if he didn't have a care in the world. Then again, maybe he didn't.

"Where do you want to eat?" I asked.

"Let me take you to the Frog & Firkin."

Knowing it was a college hangout, I responded, "Aren't we a little old for that?"

"What are you talking about? Think of the babes!" he laughed.

"Yeah, but they won't be paleo-babes . . ." I grinned.

We were almost at the restaurant when Bob asked if we could make a detour to the dry cleaner. I obliged, pulling into the driveway of Sparkle Dry Cleaners. The woman behind the counter instantly recognized Bob. As she handed him his dry cleaning, I read the name on his claim ticket. It read: "A. Dinosaur." Bob was even more out there than I thought.

At the Frog & Firkin we found the outdoor tables packed with noisy college kids. I was hoping we'd come off as a couple of hip professors rather than old fogeys. Once seated, we ordered two drafts. Our waitress, a blonde, tan cheerleader-type, gave

Bob the eye. As he chatted her up she was soon taken with his perverse charm.

While we waited for our lunch I felt I had to speak my mind. "I've got to tell you that I couldn't wait and stopped by the Co-Op this morning."

Fully enthused, Bob said, "So you saw it! What'd you think?"

"I don't know how to tell you this, Bob, but I didn't see anything. And neither did Gary, Mike, or Henry."

Bob responded, "They're all in awe of me—I find great stuff! Besides, I only brought a small section of the nest."

"Bob, what are you going to do when Peter Larson comes over? If he doesn't agree with you, you're finished."

Changing the subject, while winking at the waitress, he said, "Did I tell you I just bought 5,000 of those small Moroccan shark teeth? I buy them by the pound. When I move my exhibit over to the convention center next week, I'm going to give one to every kid. The way I look at it, I'm creating future collectors."

"I like that," I said. "But, Bob, I really think you need to—"

Bob's phone began to ring. "Fossil King!"

It was Gary Olson and Alan Komrosky. Bob had consigned them a few dinosaur bones and by the sound of things they had a buyer in their room.

"For the 'Steg' horn?" asked Bob. "What do we have it priced at? $2,500. What's he offering? $500. Okay." He paused. "Tell him it's $600 or no deal!"

Clicking off, Bob turned to me. "Sometimes you have to be tough."

We drove to the Fossil Co-Op to meet Larson. Bob was immediately accosted by a young paleontologist who panted, "Don't forget, Bob we're having dinner tonight, right?" Bob nodded and kept walking. He then gave me a world-weary *"Everyone wants a piece of me"* look.

Soon, we were at his space. Bob handed me a thin curvilinear bone from the smaller jacket and said, "I've been kicking people's butts with Gumbo!"

I inspected the miniature Triceratops bone and had to admit that it was impressive. I looked up to see Peter Larson approaching and whispered to Bob, "This is it."

The moment of truth was at hand, yet Bob appeared unfazed.

After a round of handshakes, Larson said, "All right, let's see what you've got."

Bob pointed to the smaller of the two jackets, as if he were a game show host pointing to "Door Number Three." Then he said, "Have you met Gumbo yet?"

Larson picked up the same facial bone that Bob had just shown me. Examining it with deep concentration, he turned to Bob and said, "It has juvenile texture—there's the orbital." As he continued to study it, he said tenderly, "Awww—that's a nice baby—that's a real cutie—I love this thing!"

Bob glanced over at me, making sure I was taking it all in.

Then Larson said, "I'd like to have this in our museum."

"We'll be talking," said Bob, while shooting me another look.

"So," said Larson. "Let's see the T. rex nest."

"It's coming, it's coming," said Bob. "But first, I want you to take a look at a few items I have in the trailer—they could be rex."

The next thing I knew we were out in the parking lot. The two fossil hunters opened the trailer and slowly pulled out a group of small plaster jackets. After examining the contents of each one, Larson would pronounce judgment: "The thing about rex bone is that it's so dense." Then, "I'm not sure it's bone—could be bone—but if it is, it's not theropod."

Finished with his inspection, Larson said, "You know, whatever you've got here, it would take forever to clean and prepare. I seriously think you'd be better off spending your time looking for other specimens."

Bob could have been deflated by Larson's analysis, but he wasn't. Not even after Larson closed with this zinger, "My recommendation is that you crush these rocks and turn them into parking lot gravel."

With that we walked back inside the building. The tension was mounting, at least in my mind, as we approached the larger of two plaster jackets. It was do or die. Larson bent down to conduct his final exam. I noticed his tee shirt depicted a dinosaur. Above it was the quote, "Bad to the Bone." Knife in hand, Larson began to probe. He did so with the care of a surgeon. Every few seconds he'd pause as if to confirm his diagnosis.

Then he spoke. Peter Larson, who had spent eighteen long months in prison for adhering to his principles over the greatest T. rex ever discovered, said, "I don't see any bone texture. I'm not seeing the nice shiny bone I want to see."

Without hesitation, Bob said, "It's there."

Larson continued, "It's possible you have some carbonized plant material—but I've never seen plant material associated with a theropod nest."

Maintaining his cool, Bob said, "It's really there, Pete."

Then Larson squinted and began scraping at an area along the perimeter of the jacket. He uncovered what to my eye looked like a tiny piece of bone.

Bob peered down. "There—there's some baby theropod bone!"

Larson gently pried out a sliver of fossil. He rolled it back and forth in his hand to free it of excess dirt. He even wet his finger and rubbed it on the fragment, exposing its black surface.

With awesome timing, Larson announced, "It's turtle shell—sorry Bob."

I felt awful.

Bob said nothing. He slowly walked away. He didn't slink, he just calmly walked out the door.

I went out to console him. The sun was radiating heat and

the skies were pristine. Bob stood there breathing it all in. By the look on his face he didn't need any help. His expression was almost beatific.

When I went back inside Larson came over to me. "I don't want you to get the wrong impression—we all love Bob. I have no doubt that he's going to find a great T. rex someday because of his perseverance—maybe even the first nest. Perseverance is what it takes."

Then he yelled to Bob, "I've got to go—talk to you soon." Larson left with a gentle wave.

Bob may have been bloodied but he was certainly unbowed. With a regal sigh, he looked me in the eye and said, "If Pete had dug down a bit he would have found it. I know it's there—on my mother's grave!"

I stared at him, trying to fathom his mental landscape. It had been a long haul for Bob. Endless days searching the badlands of South Dakota, dozens of false starts, countless hours of lab work, the unrelenting doubt of his peers. I continued to look at him, unsure if I should say anything. After all, what was left to be said?

Then I saw that Bob Detrich was smiling. And that slight smile grew wider, his lips parting to bravely announce, "It's not over yet! The King acquiesces to no one. It's there and I will prove it!"

CHAPTER TWENTY-EIGHT

Little Richard

Over the next six months, I kept in touch with Bob sporadically. Each discussion was filled with the usual platitudes and superlatives about his latest discovery—"They don't call me The King for nothing!"—but I gradually began to lose faith. As much as I liked and admired him, his act was starting to wear thin. So was his credibility after last year's empty nest fiasco.

Another six months passed and before I knew it, I was making plans to attend the next Gem, Mineral and Fossil Showcase of Tucson. I thought about calling Bob to schedule a dinner, but something stopped me. I didn't want to deal with all his nonsense and broken promises of having discovered yet another "T. rex." I just wanted to see the show, say hello to my friends, and buy a few fossils.

Arriving in Tucson, I dropped by the Epic Café for a quick cappuccino. That's when I ran into the dinosaur egg expert Charlie Magovern and his wife Florence. The Magoverns had driven down from Colorado to work with Henry Galiano.

After catching up on personal news, I asked, "Any word on whether Detrich's attending?"

Magovern wiped his silver beard. "I haven't heard anything. Although we're planning to do some skiing together in Boulder after the show. But like I said, I have no idea whether he's coming to Tucson."

Later that day, I drove to the Inn Suites to check out the show. I stopped by Mike Triebold's display and was immediately overwhelmed by a cast skeleton of a flying reptile known as a Pteranodon. The creature's massive wingspan reminded me we were mere Lilliputians compared to the dinosaurs. Triebold, always a class act, greeted me warmly and encouraged me not to give up my search for a T. rex.

I also chatted with his colleague Tracie, who was writing a book about the uncanny link between "chance" and making scientific discoveries—like how urinating in the wild has led to major finds. For a moment, I thought I misheard her. Then Triebold recounted the time he was out in the field and found a small fossil mammal while answering nature's call. The same thing allegedly happened to Gary Olson, leading to the discovery of the T. rex, "Ivan." Incredibly, I soon bumped into Olson in the same serendipitous way he found his dinosaur—only this time it was in an actual bathroom. Knowing he and Bob were good friends, I joked, "Any word from the King?"

"Oh, you haven't heard?"

"Heard what?"

Olson began to grin, "He may have actually done it."

"Done what?"

"Found a T. rex."

"Seriously?" I asked.

"It's true. He's still a long way from a complete skeleton, but he may have ten percent of the animal."

Since a T. rex is composed of approximately 300 bones that meant that Bob had uncovered around thirty of them. Most paleontologists considered that to be the minimum before you could be credited with having discovered a Tyrannosaurus rex.

Still stunned, I asked, "Have you seen it?"

"Yeah, he showed me three beautiful claws—really nice. He also has a rex fibula and maybe the end of a tibia." Then Olson added, "You know Bob—always selling the sizzle rather than the steak—but this time he may have gotten the flavor and the bones."

Taking a break, I found a seat at one of the tables surrounding the pool. I sipped a cold beer and thought about Bob's potential find. If true, his claim to be the Fossil King would no longer ring hollow. His coronation would finally take place.

I knew Bob usually hunted with Stan Sacrison, so I called Buffalo, South Dakota and got his mother, Ruth, on the phone, "Hi, Mrs. Sacrison—it's Richard Polsky—Bob Detrich's friend. Is your son home?"

"Yes, he's out in the garage."

Forgetting how cold it must have been that time of year, I asked, "Could you please go get him?"

Ruth hesitated and said, "It's all the way outside in the snow."

"I'd really appreciate it."

With an audible groan, she said, "I guess I could."

A minute later, Stan got on the phone, sounding rather grumpy, "Hello?"

"Hey, Stan, what have you been up to?"

"Not much. Mostly doing some metal detecting—finding a few Mercury dimes around old junk piles—nothing great."

I asked, "Have you retired from dinosaur hunting?"

"No, just taking a break."

"So I understand you and Bob may have scored bigtime."

"You mean the claws?" said Stan.

"Right—did you guys find any other rex bones?" I asked.

"Uh, let's see—yeah, we found part of a maxilla."

"Any teeth in it?"

"Nope, but whatever is out there is pretty scattered—it's possible when we go back we'll find some teeth."

Then I asked the big question, "Does Bob really have the necessary thirty bones?"

There was silence. "Oh, I don't know. Let's see . . . you've got some claws, the jaw section, parts from some leg bones, maybe some ribs . . . hmm . . . come to think of it, he might have enough—and like I said there could be more out there."

"So what do you think he'll name it?" I queried.

"He told the land owner he might call it 'Jack'—after my dad."

Hanging up with Stan, I excitedly called Bob. After trying all three of his numbers, I finally got through. Recognizing my number on his caller ID, he yelled, "Richarrrrrrd! Are you at the show? Are they talking about me?"

"They sure are! Are you coming?"

"I'm on my way—don't worry, I'll be there tomorrow."

"Why the delay? Why aren't you here now?"

"Hey—I'm building the anticipation. You know how the Rolling Stones are always intentionally late for their concerts? It gets the audience all revved up waiting for them to take the stage!"

Great, I thought, *now he thinks he's a rock star.*

"I'll call you when I get in," said Bob, signing off.

I returned to the fair, planning to stop by Henry Galiano's room. As I strode across the lawn, I spotted his wife Debbie reclining on a lounge chair, soaking up the sun's seventy-degree rays.

"Hi, Deb. It must feel good to be out of New York right now."

She nodded appreciatively. "When I left yesterday, it was all of twelve degrees."

I walked inside, found Henry Galiano's room and was confronted by a glass case containing two jaw sections from a T. rex. Each piece was the color of a brackish stream, about two-feet long, and fully lined with curved teeth. Upon closer inspection, I could tell the teeth were fabricated.

Henry got off the phone and came over to greet me, "Hey good to see you."

"Nice rex jaws—what are you asking for them?"

"They're $150,000," said Henry.

"Even though the teeth are casts?"

"The jaw bone's all real and it's pretty rare to find part of the skull—especially jaws," he explained.

"How's the market for rex material in general? Still strong?"

"Seems to be," Henry concurred. "You probably heard Gary Olson sold Ivan for $600,000 to an institution in Wichita."

"Wasn't he asking a million?"

"Hey, you can ask whatever you want. But remember, they only had forty percent of the bone and no skull. I think they did pretty well."

Roaming the fair in search of rex specimens, I came upon the Black Hills Institute's grand installation in the hotel's ballroom. Although they'd brought their usual unsurpassed inventory of iridescent ammonites from South Dakota, it was something else that dazzled my eye.

I was drawn in by an eighteen-inch Stegosaurus horn impaled by a chocolate brown rex tooth, about two-inches long. You could tell the tooth had once popped out of its victim's cavity, but was expertly repositioned by the preparator. The Larson brothers were asking only $8,500 for this remnant of what had undoubtedly been a fierce prehistoric battle. I seriously thought about making them an offer.

I hung out at the show for another two hours, marveling at how the Moroccan dealers were seemingly taking over the fossil business. Against my better judgment, I asked one of them for a price on a "plate" of fossil shark teeth. It was a foot-long slab of off-white limestone, spiked with an assortment of two-inch long teeth whose cream-colored hue provided a pleasing contrast. Upon closer inspection, you could tell the teeth were glued into place to create a superior but unnatural composition. The dealer tried to talk me into signing up for a fossil hunting expedition in his country—only $1,800 plus airfare.

When I inquired, "Is it safe?"

He gave me a wicked grin, "But of course."

Walking away, I could just see myself trapped in a Moroccan prison living the *Midnight Express* ordeal.

That night, I fell asleep with visions of a "fossil bust" in a foreign land. When I awoke, I called Bob and made plans to have lunch together. As I drove to meet him at the appointed time, I made a quick detour to the Fossil Co-Op, to do a little reconnaissance.

I walked past a dealer's space crammed with cut and polished amethyst geodes and cathedrals. A cathedral is a vertical geode, sometimes as tall as a man, which resembles an imaginary fairy's grotto. You could see why "New Agers" were big buyers of these Brazilian crystal-lined "caves" formed from volcanic activity.

I found the empty space where Bob had set up last year. Gone was the plaster jacket that had contained the alleged T. rex nest. When I spoke with the manager of the Co-Op, he explained that Bob wasn't exhibiting this year. Instead, he decided to come to Tucson to socialize and share news of his T. rex skeleton discovery, and bask in its glow.

After purchasing a small geode, and watching a video on how they were mined, I took off to meet Bob for lunch at the college hangout, the Frog & Firkin, our rendezvous of a year ago.

I almost didn't recognize Bob. He had grown a beard since I last saw him. We embraced and then found a table, ordering a round of Guinness Black and Tans.

"The return of the conquering hero!" I cried.

"You got that right!" laughed Bob.

He then opened a cardboard box and carefully removed three fossil claws, one at a time. "Here's the baby that got the ball rolling," said Bob, as he handed me a claw—the same one found on the sheriff's property in Buffalo, *where I helped dig.*

Instantly, a Niagara of memories washed over me. I was back in the field, excavating alongside Bob, Stan, and Bucky Derflinger. I was covered in mud, lost in the moment, sifting through layers of fossil yielding sedimentary rock. I was a dinosaur hunter. Though I may not have been the one who found the actual claw that day, *I was part of the expedition that did.*

As I continued to daydream, Bob brought me back to reality when he extracted two more curved fossil talons from a box and said, "These guys are about death and carnage—it really gets your imagination going."

The claws were incredible and definitely from a T. rex. They were around five-inches-long, frayed by time, but still full of life. *Vindication at last.* I grew animated, gesturing with extended hands. "Tell me how you found them."

"Remember when we were out on the sheriff's land?"

"Oh yeah, when Bucky found that turtle shell and you thought it was rex bone," I said, purposely giving him a hard time.

Bob grimaced. "I'll bet he's not laughing now! Anyway, I was back out there again with Stan and John Carter. I was blading with the Bobcat and the two of them were searching the ground. Then I heard a loud clink. I think it was Carter who yelled out, 'Looky here!' I got off the cat and he handed me a claw. It was a bit fractured, but we were able to glue it back together. We also uncovered another bone that could be a metatarsal, plus lots of pieces of skull."

All of this sounded too good to be true. I didn't want to rain on his parade, but felt like I had to ask him some hard questions.

"So who have you shown this material to?"

"Fred Nuss has seen some of it," he said. "Pete Larson has seen the claws."

"What did Larson say?"

Bob grinned from ear to ear. "Oh, he's intimidated!"

I shook my head. "Are these hand or foot claws?"

"Definitely foot—they're way too big to have come from a T. rex's forearms."

"Are they for sale?"

"No way—it would be like cutting up a Van Gogh and selling parts of it," he said, sounding almost indignant.

Our waitress brought the pizza, a deep dish pesto pie, heavy on the pine nuts. I looked at Bob as he cut a hefty slice, deftly depositing it on his plate. Since we were sitting in almost the same booth as a year ago, I couldn't help but reflect on his change of fortune. What a difference a year made. Suddenly, he was living up to his own lofty expectations.

Bob's T. rex journey wasn't over; it was just beginning. Even though he and his team had been working for weeks on a surface dig, there was still more work to be done and hopefully more bone to be recovered. There was no guarantee that Bob's dinosaur would be certified as a legitimate rex and take its place on the list of forty plus discoveries. But it felt possible.

In theory, a paleontologist could look at the minimum requirement of thirty rex bones and say, "Three of these fragments are actually from the same bone—sorry, you only have twenty-eight." It could also work the other way and two fragments could, upon further study, turn out to be two individual bones. Time would tell.

Bob scratched his head. "When I showed Pete Larson the claws, he commented they were smaller than Bucky's. There's a good chance this is a juvenile rex—a real rarity."

"I've been dying to ask you—what are you going to name it?"

Bob heaved a great sigh, "Everyone's been asking me that. I thought about taking all the credit and naming it after myself. But you know that's not my style. I've been considering calling it 'Jack,' after the Bonehead Brothers' father. But you know, now that we're sitting here—enjoying this fine pizza together—and given you helped work the site—maybe I'll name it *Richard*."

I just looked at him, not sure if he was kidding.

Then Bob said, "But the more I think about it, since it's probably a juvenile, I think I'll call it *Little Richard!*"

I grinned and thought, *Maybe I'd be watching myself on the Discovery Channel after all.*

"That's it," repeated Bob, with a gleam in his eye, "*Little Richard.*"

EPILOGUE

Bob Detrich lives the life of a dinosaur hunter, a life I once envisioned for myself as a younger man. For most of us, there's a predictability to how our days unfold. Not Bob's day. There is always serendipity to it. He could be out in the field for weeks on end—even months—and find nothing. Or he could discover a major Triceratops and walk away with hundreds of thousands of dollars—which he once did.

Unfortunately, the dinosaur business is becoming a "dinosaur." When Peter Larson expressed his concern over the lack of young people entering the field, he was voicing the truth. While there's a distinction to be drawn between professional paleontologists and commercial collectors, both fields offer dwindling prospects.

If you go the professional route and wind up with a rare position at an institution, your duties are primarily curatorial. A typical day is about maintenance of the collection and scientific research. Due to shrinking funds, collecting trips are infrequent. On those rare forays into the field, you're usually searching for fossils to support your theories, rather than pursuing attention-getting skeletons for display. Despite the prestige and relative financial security, it's hardly an exciting lifestyle. Certainly not one that's likely to attract the next generation in the current high-tech era.

Those who become commercial collectors are in it because they enjoy an independent lifestyle. They're unwilling to trade authentic adventure, and an occasional shot at glory, for the career stability of their professional counterparts. Unfortunately, there is a tsunami of factors working against these individuals. For one thing, as more museums become filled with dinosaur skeletons, they've begun to run out of space. After all, a few dinosaurs go a long way.

The emphasis on original bones isn't what it used to be. Due to shrinking budgets, institutions have increasingly sought out high-quality casts. Factor in the increasing vigilance by the government monitoring public lands, price comparison-shopping on eBay, the consolidation of the business into only a few mega-dealers, and you're talking about an iffy future.

Participating in Bob's world exposed me to the precariousness of his existence. It also made me reflect on my decision not to pursue a career in paleontology—the road not taken.

Back in 1973, I enrolled at Miami University (Oxford, Ohio) as a geology major. Unlike many incoming freshmen, I had a sense of direction. During orientation week, I joined the geological society, spent time at the geology museum, and even went fossil hunting with a fellow geology student. When I met with some professors and shared stories of my recent museum internship at the Cleveland Museum of Natural History, they were duly impressed and told me how pleased they were to have me in the department. So far, everything was going according to plan.

Then a funny thing happened on my way to a degree. I never realized that majoring in geology was actually majoring in *science*. That meant required courses in physics, trigonometry, and chemistry, which were among the toughest classes offered. No matter how hard I tried, I couldn't keep up. I had always been a poor math student. By the end of my first week at Miami, I knew I was in over my head. At the conclusion of the second week, I was on my way to flunking out.

After some desperate thinking, I had an epiphany: my interest in geology had nothing to do with a love of science. It was really about my passion for aesthetics. There was something about how the curvilinear shape of a fossil brachiopod rivaled the organic forms of a Henry Moore bronze. I viewed fossils as pieces of sculpture rather than objects that could help us determine how life on our planet evolved.

Once I understood the truth about myself, I knew I had to change directions. I became an art major. When I called my parents with the news, their reaction was predictable. My father drove five hours from Cleveland to Oxford to talk to me in person. This was too serious a discussion to have over the phone.

When Dad arrived it was already dinnertime. We headed uptown to a restaurant called Al & Larry's. I distinctly recall my Dad asking me, "Do you want a beer?" It was the first beer with my father, a serious rite of passage in a young man's life.

Then we got into it. He gave me a well thought-out speech about not ruining my life. My father spoke from experience. He had originally been a pharmacy major at St. John's College. Then he hit a speed bump. He couldn't get through chemistry and switched over to marketing. Like father, like son.

That evening, it all came down to a single concern: "What are you going to *do* with a degree in art?"

At the age of eighteen, you're blinded by optimism. Despite the odds, I envisioned becoming a successful sculptor. I spent the next four years studying art and graduated with a BFA degree. A few years into my career revealed that my talent was no better than ordinary. Still, I hoped my passion would sustain me. To pay for my art habit, I worked for a gallery and learned that I had a knack for art dealing.

In my second great moment of truth, I quit making art and opened my own space in downtown San Francisco in 1984. The gallery prospered—we even did a Warhol show—and I later became a private dealer. Yet, there was always the nagging doubt over whether I'd made the right choice. I didn't want to live a life of regret. Things came full circle when I contacted Henry Galiano, triggering my search for a T. rex and a possible solution to this vexing question.

My experiences with Bob Detrich told me that fossils would always remain a great love, but I was glad I never became a paleontologist. While Bob was more extreme than most of his colleagues, his rough and tumble lifestyle was typical. So was his tolerance for risk. His quarry was many millions of years old, hidden in hundreds of miles of badlands. Yet it had to be uncovered in excellent condition, legally collected, and rare enough to be in demand. As Mike Triebold said, it had to have "horns, claws, or fangs."

On a daily basis Bob psyched himself into believing he would land the big one. He was a "dinosauraholic." I came to understand that finding a dinosaur—a saleable dinosaur—was really like trying to beat Las Vegas. And we all know how often that happens. Who could live their life based on something that might or might not exist? Personally, I couldn't spin the wheel of fortune each day and hope it landed on an icon depicting a giant skull with nasty teeth.

Bob Detrich was willing to spin that wheel every day, whether in the field or in his dreams. Which was what made him the once and future Fossil King.

Acknowledgements

I have to hand it to publisher Barnaby Conrad III . . . you found a way, old buddy. I wish to acknowledge Paulette Millichap of Council Oak Books. Maurice Kanbar deserves to be singled out for all his support. A hearty thank you to Henry Galiano for acting as my liaison to the world of dinosaur hunters. Thanks to Sonja Bolle for transforming my approach to writing this book. And a final expression of gratitude to my agent Bonnie Nadell of Hill Nadell Literary Agency for your wisdom and patience.

The following individuals distinguished themselves by contributing to the adventure: Tracie Bennit, Japheth Boyce, Bob and Linda Carroll, Kathleen Critchett, Bucky Derflinger, Richard Gray, Diana Hensley, Jared Hudson, Bill and Denise Kane, Neal Larson, Peter Larson, Tom Lindgren, Gary Olson, Charlie Magovern, Jonathan Marshall and Lorrie Goldin, Marlit Polsky, David Redden, Stan Sacrison, Steve Sacrison, Walter Stein, Mike Triebold, Joe Wachs, and Maurice and Darlene Williams.

And, of course, Bob Detrich.

SOURCES

Alvarez, Walter. *T. rex and the Crater of Doom*. Princeton University Press, 1997.

Bakker, Robert. *Raptor Red*. Bantam Books, 1995.

Davis, Buddy, and Liston, Mike, and Whitmore, John. *The Great Alaska Dinosaur Adventure*. Master Books, 1998.

Duffy, Patrick and Lofgren, Lois, "Jurassic Farce." *South Dakota Law Review*, Volume 39, Issue 3.

Fiffer, Steve. *Tyrannosaurus Sue*. W. H. Freeman and Company, 2000.

Fredericks, Mike. *Prehistoric Times* (magazine). #67, Aug./Sept., 2004.

Gayard-Valy. *Fossils: Evidence of Vanished Worlds*. Harry N. Abrams, 1994.

Horner, John and Lessen, Don. *The Complete T. rex*. Simon & Schuster, 1993.

Larson, Peter and Donnan, Kristin. *Bones Rock!*, Invisible Cities Press, 2004.

Larson, Peter and Donnan, Kristin. *Rex Appeal*. Invisible Cities Press, 2002.

Long, John. *The Dinosaur Dealers*. Allen & Unwin, 2002.

Michard, Jean-Guy. *The Reign of Dinosaurs*, Harry N. Abrams, 1992.

Mitchell, W. J. T., *The Last Dinosaur Book*. The University of Chicago Press, 1998.

Natural History. Bonhams & Butterfields, auction catalog. Los Angeles, May 16, 2004.

Preston, Douglas J. *Dinosaurs in the Attic*. St. Martin's Press, 1986.

Psihoyos, Louie. *Hunting Dinosaurs*. Random House, 1994.

Renz, Mark. *Megladon: Hunting the Hunter*. Paleo Press, 2002.

Sotheby's. Tyrannosaurus rex, auction catalog. New York, October 4, 1997.

Stein, Walter. *So You Want to Dig Dinosaurs?* Dragons Claw Press, 2001.

Svarney, Thomas and Barnes-Svarney, Patricia. *The Handy Dinosaur Answer Book*. Visible Ink Press, 2000.

Webster, Donovan. "A Dinosaur Named Sue." *National Geographic*, June, 1999.

100 Years of Tyrannosaurus rex. (abstracts from symposium) Black Hills Museum of Natural History, 2005.